DATE DUE

			PRINTED IN U.S.A.

Walt Disney

Walt Disney

A Biography by Barbara Ford

Walker and Company
New York

First published in the United States of America in 1989
by the Walker Publishing Company, Inc.

Published simultaneously in Canada by Thomas Allen &
Son Canada, Limited, Markham, Ontario.

Ford, Barbara.
　Walt Disney / written by Barbara Ford.
　　p.　cm.
　Bibliography: p.
　Includes index.
　Summary: Follows the life and career of the man who fulfilled his creative dreams
by founding a motion picture empire.
　ISBN 0-8027-6864-4.　ISBN 0-8027-6865-2 (lib. bdg.)
　[1. Disney, Walt, 1901–1966—Juvenile literature.　2. Animators-1901–1966.　2.
Motion pictures—Biography.]　I. Title.
NC1766.U52D537 1989
791.43'092'4—dc19
[B]
[92]　　　　　　　　　　　　　　　　　　　　　　　　　　　88-29328
　　　　　　　　　　　　　　　　　　　　　　　　　　　　　CIP
　　　　　　　　　　　　　　　　　　　　　　　　　　　　　AC

Printed in the United States of America

10　9　8　7

Book design by Laurie McBarnette

Walt Disney

Kansas Avenue, Marceline, Mo. 1910 *Before*

Mason

CATER'S
OPERA HOUSE

The main street of Marceline, Missouri, in 1910, the year Walt left.—RUTH HERYFORD COLLECTION

ethodist ch
ilt in 1910
emple 1923

Chapter One

A farm! Five-year-old Walter Elias Disney had spent his whole life in the big city of Chicago, but now his family was going to live on a farm! He twisted restlessly on the seat of the horse-drawn buggy as it rattled slowly down the dirt road outside Marceline, Missouri. There were some automobiles in Chicago in 1906, but out here in the Missouri countryside, horses still provided most of the transportation.

Finally the buggy, which belonged to one of their new neighbors, stopped before a one-story house.

Walt leaned eagerly out of the buggy. It was spring, and the apple and plum trees near the house were all in blossom. In front of the house was a weeping willow and behind it were green hills. It was the most beautiful place, Walt thought, that he had ever seen.

Walt, his little sister Ruth, his thirteen-year-old brother Roy, and his mother spent a happy week camping out at the farm, waiting for Walt's father and two oldest brothers to arrive. Flora Disney, a lively, even-tempered woman, read the children stories and took part in their games. Elias Disney and Walt's two teen-aged brothers, Ray and Hubert, arrived a week later in a wagon with the family furniture.

Elias had been a carpenter and builder in Chicago. In fact, he had built the family's first home. But now he planned to cultivate the forty-eight-acre farm with the help of his four sons. Elias was a hard worker, and he soon had everyone in the family except little Ruth working hard, too. The older boys worked in the fields with their father. Flora cooked and cleaned and made butter, which she sold in the nearby town of Marceline. She also made most of the family's clothes. Little Walt took care of the animals: chickens, pigeons, ducks, and pigs.

Caring for the animals was a big job for a boy Walt's age, but he liked the work. He gave all the animals names, even though his brothers laughed at him. Whenever he saw one of his charges, he talked to it by name. If he didn't, he felt, the animal would be offended.

"Hi Effie!" he would call. "Hello Elmer. How's the old foot this morning, Mortimer—frozen?"

Some of the animals became his special friends. One hen, Martha, would come when he called her name and lay an egg right in his hand. And Porker, the biggest sow, or female pig, would let him ride on her back. Of course she always threw him off into the duck pond, but that was part of the game. Walt could tell that from the mischievous way she looked at him as he picked himself up from the water.

Walt liked the rabbits and deer and other wild animals that lived on or near the farm, too. During the first week they were at the farm, Roy and Walt watched some rabbits in the fields near the farm. Roy shot one of them with an airgun. Flora made a delicious rabbit stew that night, but Walt wouldn't eat it. He never went hunting, even though it was a popular pastime among most of the boys in the neighborhood.

Running the farm kept the Disneys busy most of the time, but Walt still found time for fun. The farm was near the little town of Marceline, which had a population of about five thousand people when the Disneys arrived. It was on the main line of the Santa Fe Railroad, and the tracks passed near the Disney farm. Walt liked to ride into Marceline in the horse-drawn wagon and walk down Main Street. There was lots to interest a small boy on Main Street—shops like the haberdashery, where men's hats were sold, the barber shop, and the general store, where you could buy anything from clothing to food. There was a firehouse, too, and the railroad station, where someone always seemed to be going or coming.

There were other ways to have fun, too. In hot weather, Walt and his friends would swim in a pool near the Santa Fe Railroad tracks. Afterward they would fish or catch frogs. And sometimes Walt would just watch the big steam engine pulling long strings of freight or passenger cars on the railroad tracks, or the new automobiles chugging by on the dirt road in front of the farmhouse.

Little Ruth, two years younger than Walt, often tagged along after her big brother. When the brother and sister played in the fields near the creek, Walt, a daring youngster, would insist that they return home through the pasture where the big bull was kept. The bull always chased them, and Ruth, with her short legs, was always afraid it was going to catch her. Walt would help her scramble over the pasture fence as the bull, hoofs pounding, bore down on them.

Elias and Flora were sociable, and relatives and friends filled the house in Marceline. One of the children's favorite guests was Uncle Mike, an engineer on the Santa Fe. He worked the route between Marceline and Fort Madison, Iowa, and he often stayed overnight. Whenever he did, he brought a bag of candy for the children. Since Elias never allowed his children to buy sweets, they always looked forward to Uncle Mike's visits.

But Walt's favorite relative was Uncle Ed. Some people

Ruth and Walt ages 5 and 7, in Marceline.—COURTESY OF RUTH
DISNEY BEECHER

said Uncle Ed was "retarded," but Walt didn't know what that meant. All he knew was that Uncle Ed brought them candy, too—and chewing gum! Elias Disney disapproved of chewing gum even more than candy, so Walt would chew his gum when his father wasn't around and then park it carefully under the porch railing so he could chew it again the next day.

But the real reason Walt loved Uncle Ed was that he shared Walt's love of animals. When Ed visited, he and Walt would explore the farm and the fields around it. Ed would get field mice to nestle in his pockets and wild birds to sit on his shoulder. Walt called his uncle Uncle Elf, because the small man with the lined face looked like an elf to his nephew.

Walt didn't start school in Marceline until he was almost seven years old, because Elias wanted him to wait until Ruth could attend school with him. The Park School, which was about a mile away from the Disneys' house, was a brand-new school in 1908, when Walt and Ruth entered it. The brick building stood two stories high and had eight teachers. It included both a grade school and a high school. Walt spent two years there and at some point during that time he carved his initials on one of the wooden desks.

One day, when the elder Disneys had taken the wagon to town, Walt discovered a closed barrel of fresh tar next to the house. It was being used for repairs. Walt suggested to his sister that they use the gooey substance to paint pictures on the side of the house.

"Will it come off?" asked Ruth.

Walt assured her it would and the two went to work. He

drew houses, she contributed zigzags. Before long, they discovered that dry tar will *not* come off. Elias was furious when he returned home. The tar pictures stayed on the side of the house.

Most of Walt's drawings were done on paper. About the time he started school, he started to draw the animals on the farm and in the fields around it. There was no paper to spare in the Disney household, so he sketched animals on toilet paper and wrapping paper. Relatives admired Walt's work and his Aunt Margaret from Kansas City sent him drawing materials.

During these years, a special bond grew between Walt and his brother Roy. Roy was eight years older than Walt but the two always seemed to understand each other. Sometimes Roy would go swimming with Walt and the two would roam the fields around the farm, observing animals and plants. When Roy was able to earn some money by working for another farmer or in town, he would buy Walt a toy or give him money to buy special treats.

Roy wasn't happy on the farm, though. Probably no one but Walt and his little sister were. The farm was beautiful but it was too small to support a family, even with the whole family working. The older boys soon grew tired of so much labor for so little return, particularly since Elias was often in a bad humor. Elias was quick-tempered and irritable, especially when he was worried. And now he was worried. He had begun to realize that the small farm was not economical.

Finally, Ray and Hubert, the oldest boys, had had enough. They saved some money and one night climbed out the window with their suitcases and took a train to Chicago.

The loss of his sons was one of a series of blows for Elias. A short time before, his pigs had come down with swine fever and even Walt's favorite, Porker, had to be destroyed. Then a drought forced Elias to mortgage the farm. And shortly after his sons left, Elias contracted typhoid fever from the well water. Luckily, the rest of the family escaped the disease. Elias survived, but he was in poor health for years.

Roy, who was only sixteen, couldn't run the farm himself. In the winter of 1908–09, Walt and Roy drove a farm wagon all over the area, tacking up notices that advertised the farm for sale.

During that same winter, when Walt was eight years old, he earned the first money he had ever made from drawing. His mother had used some of the money she made selling butter to buy a him a sketchbook and he had filled it with drawings of Porker, Martha, and the other animals. The local physician, Dr. Caleb Sherwood, admired the sketchbook and asked Walt to draw a picture of his horse, Rupert. He paid Walt fifty cents for the sketch.

The auction of the farm produced enough money to pay off the mortgage and other debts, with something left over. Roy, Walt, and Ruth stayed in Marceline with their mother so they could finish the school year. Then, in the summer of 1910, the Disneys boarded the train for Kansas City, Missouri, where Elias was already living. Walt had spent less than five years in Marceline, but he would never forget it or the animals and people he knew there.

In Kansas City, Elias had bought a modest two-story home that he remodeled using his carpentry skills. He supported his family with a newspaper delivery service. Since he was in poor health, he couldn't deliver the papers himself; that job was up to Walt and Roy. Every morning, they were up by 3:30 A.M. to begin their rounds. Elias wouldn't allow them to throw the papers. In warm weather, they had to take each one up to the door and place it there, unfolded, with a stone to weigh it down. In cold weather, they had to open the storm door and put the paper inside.

As soon as the boys had delivered the morning papers, they would rush home, have breakfast, and go to school. After school, they delivered the evening paper. On Sundays there was only one paper, but it weighed more than all the daily ones put together. Sometimes Walt was so sleepy that he took a nap in the corridor of one of the apartment houses where he delivered papers. All the money the two boys earned from delivering newspapers went to their father.

Sometimes Walt would have a nightmare. He would wake up, sweating and terrified, having dreamed that he had failed to deliver a paper to some customer.

Roy endured this routine for two years. Then he, too, slipped away in the night. Walt was the only one Roy told about his plans.

Now twelve-year-old Walt and ten-year-old Ruth were the only children left at home. Walt wanted money of his own, so he found new customers for his newspapers and kept the money they gave him. He had to get up at 3:00 A.M. instead of 3:30 to deliver the extra papers. He also earned money by sweeping out the candy store across the street from his school and by delivering prescriptions for a drugstore. He spent much of his pocket money on candy.

Flora and Elias Disney around 1911 in Kansas City.—COURTESY OF
RUTH DISNEY BEECHER

Young Walt had plenty of energy and his busy schedule didn't seem to affect his health. But his schoolwork at the Benton School on Benton Boulevard in Kansas City suffered. His teachers complained that he didn't pay attention. Not all of Walt's troubles at school were due to lack at attention, though. Often he didn't carry out assigned work, his teachers reported. He did what he wanted to do instead.

On one occasion, the fourth grade was assigned to draw a bowl of flowers. Walt set to work enthusiastically, but when the teacher looked at his drawing, she saw that each flower had a face and arms. She reprimanded him for not following the assignment.

Walt's real interest lay outside schoolwork. In Kansas City, he discovered the world of professional entertainment. Movie houses offered the latest silent films, and vaudeville houses showcased live performers. A typical vaudeville "bill" consisted of a number of short acts that might include anything from a magic act to trained animals. Comics, singers, and dancers were staples on most bills. Vaudeville performers traveled from town to town, presenting the same act.

But it was movies that made the biggest impression on Walt. Sometime during his years in Kansas City, he saw a film version of the fairy tale *Snow White* starring actress Marguerite Clark. It was based on her successful stage play. Walt watched, entranced, as the young, dark-haired Marguerite Clark "died" on the screen and then, miraculously, came to life again. Like all films in those days, *Snow White* was "silent"; the dialogue was in subtitles.

Walt saw the films made by the famous comedians of the silent film era, too. Charlie Chaplin, the best-known film actor of that day, so impressed Walt that he and a friend worked up acts based on Chaplin's film characters. The two boys put on the acts at Benton School. Walt's most popular act involved his pretending to be a photographer. But instead of taking pictures with his "camera," Walt would douse his subjects with a stream of water. Then he would produce a "photograph": a caricature of the student he had drawn himself.

Walt and his friend put on this act in a contest at a local theater and won fourth prize: twenty-five cents.

Walt tried more serious dramatic presentations, too. When he was in fifth grade at Benton School, Walt devised an Abraham Lincoln costume from an old hat, a false beard, and a "wart" that he pasted on his chin. On Lincoln's Birthday, Walt stood in front of his classmates, wearing his costume, and recited the Gettysburg Address. Walt's teacher was very impressed. She asked the principal to hear Walt and he, too, was impressed. He took Walt to each of the classes, where the boy repeated his performance.

After that, it became an annual event for Walt to don his costume and recite the Gettysburg Address in front of each class.

Walt enjoyed performing before an audience, but he liked drawing even better. His skill as an artist was improving. When Ruth was sick, he made a series of pictures for her that looked as though they were moving when she flipped rapidly through them. He copied the cartoons in one of his father's magazines. He drew cartoons of the customers at the local barbershop. The barber hung them up and cut Walt's hair for free.

When he was fourteen, Walt began taking lessons on Saturday morning at the Kansas City Art Institute. By this time, he was sure of what he wanted to be: a cartoonist.

Elias didn't approve wholeheartedly of Walt's ambition, even though he paid for Walt's art lessons. If Walt wanted to go into the arts, argued Elias, why not learn to play a musical instrument so he could get a job in a band? Elias worried that Walt would not make a living at drawing. Elias himself played the violin, and he encouraged his children to play musical instruments, too. He had recently bought Ruth a piano. Now he brought out his old violin and insisted that Walt play it.

To please his father, Walt scraped away at the instrument, hating every minute of it. Later, Ruth remembered that he learned only one song: "Of Thee I Sing."

At this age, Walt was as big as his father and much stronger. But Elias was still ordering Walt to the basement every time the teen-ager was "impertinent" or disobeyed one of Elias's rules. There Elias would beat his son with a leather strap. Roy was visiting on one occasion when Elias ordered Walt to the basement.

"You're fourteen years old," Roy told Walt. "Don't take it anymore."

When Elias met his son in the basement, he raised his hand with the strap but Walt grabbed his father's wrist. Elias struggled feebly but Walt was much stronger than he was. When Walt saw tears appear in Elias's eyes, he loosened his grip. Father and son climbed back up the stairs. Elias never tried to beat his son again.

Walt's relations with his mother were much smoother,

thanks to Flora's even temper. She never displayed anger. All the Disney children were strong-willed, according to Ruth, so rearing five of them on Elias's modest earnings was no easy task. On one occasion, Flora confided to Ruth that boys were harder to raise than girls. She was thinking, no doubt, of her sons' struggles with Elias.

In 1917, the restless Elias decided to make another move—this time back to Chicago, Walt's birthplace. He sold his newspaper route and invested the money in a Chicago jelly factory. Walt was going to graduate from Benton School in June, so he stayed behind with a friend. After his graduation, Walt took a summer job on the railroad, selling food and newspapers to passengers.

It turned out to be one of the best summers Walt ever had. Wearing a blue uniform with gold buttons, he traveled back and forth from Kansas City to towns and cities in a number of midwestern states. Sometimes the engineer let him ride in the cab in the front of the train, where he could see the scenery rushing up to him. Walt's summer job gave him a lifelong love of trains.

At the end of the summer, Walt joined his family in Chicago. He entered McKinley High School and drew cartoons for the school newspaper. After school, he studied cartooning at the Chicago Academy of Fine Arts, paying for the lessons himself with money he saved from his part-time jobs. He held several jobs during the school year, one on Chicago's elevated railroad.

Walt didn't have much time for a social life, but somehow he found time to fall in love with a McKinley student, Su.

In the summer of 1917, while Walt was selling food and

newspapers on the railroad, the United States had entered World War I. Roy and Walt's other brothers joined the armed forces. In 1918, when Walt was sixteen, he lied about his age and joined the American Red Cross as an ambulance driver. He had spent only one year in high school, and he never returned.

Walt was still in the United States when the war ended in 1918. Many American troops were still overseas, however, and the Red Cross needed more drivers. Walt was shipped to France. Su, impressed with Walt's patriotism, promised to wait for him. Walt drove ambulances and trucks in France but, as always, he found time to do what he liked best—draw. He made posters for the barracks where he and his army buddies lived, and he sent back letters illustrated with cartoons to the school newspaper.

He also adopted a dog, which he named for Carey Orr, a cartoonist on the *Chicago Tribune* and Walt's hero.

One of Walt's friends took Carey back to Chicago and promised to keep the dog until Walt arrived. By the fall of 1919, Walt was back in the United States. In Chicago, he learned that Su had married three months before, an event she had never mentioned in her letters. Walt took Su's picture out of his wallet and tore it up. Then he went to see the friend who had kept his dog. The dog had died, the friend told him.

Walt's job hunt didn't go any better. When he applied to Carey Orr for a job as a cartoonist, the veteran cartoonist was not impressed with Walt's work. In any case, there were no openings on the *Tribune*. When Elias heard the story, he advised his son to forget about cartooning and take a job at his jelly factory.

"I want to be an artist," Walt insisted.

But Elias still disapproved of art as a career. An artist, he said, couldn't make any money. The next day, Walt, like his brothers, left home for good. He joined Roy and one of his other brothers in the family's old house in Kansas City. Walt applied as a cartoonist to the *Kansas City Star*, whose papers he had delivered for so many years. But there were no openings there, either.

Roy had heard about an opening in a small commercial art studio, so Walt applied. He got the job. He was eighteen years old, and at last he had a job as an artist, if not a cartoonist.

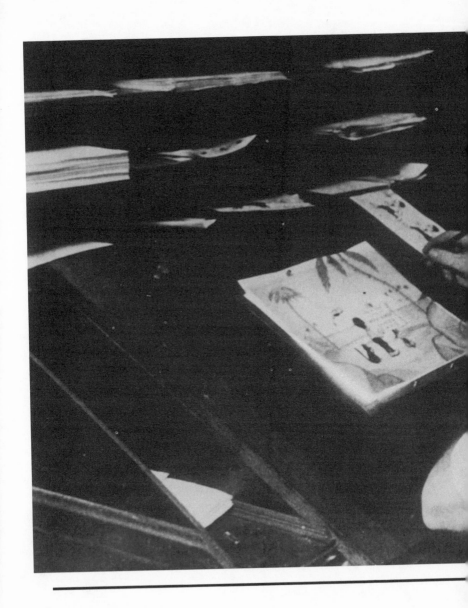

A Walt without a mustache at his desk at the Kansas City Film Ad
Company in Kansas City. One of his drawings is on the desk.
—Kansas City Star

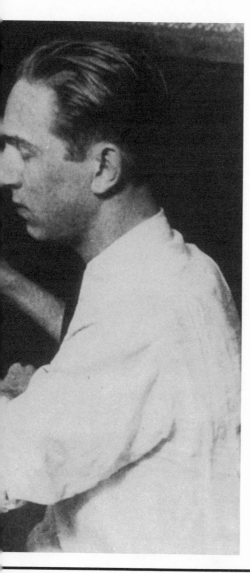

Chapter Two

The advertising firm Walt Disney joined in Kansas City in 1919 was named the Pesman-Rubin Commercial Art Studio. Walt had to make drawings of agricultural implements, which didn't interest him very much, but he also had a chance to draw farm animals. For one of his first assignments, he drew a cow licking a salt block sold by the Carey Salt Company.

Just before Pesman-Rubin hired Walt, they had hired another eighteen-year-old, Ubbe Iwerks. Ubbe's curious name was Dutch; he was the son of a man who had come to the United States from Holland. Ubbe was very shy but he was already a skilled artist. He showed Walt some of the tricks he had learned to make drawings look more professional.

Both young men had been hired to help Pesman-Rubin deal with the Christmas rush, and soon after Christmas they were both let go. Walt suggested to Ubbe that they form their own art studio. Ubbe, who needed money to help his family, agreed. After Walt persuaded Ubbe to shorten his name to Ub Iwerks, they named the firm Iwerks-Disney. They opened for business in an office that belonged to their first client, who traded them the rent for artwork.

At first the new business did surprisingly well. Walt discovered that he was a born salesman, and soon he had convinced a number of clients to buy artwork from Iwerks-Disney. The partners were able to afford a bigger office. Then, in the spring of 1920, Walt saw an ad in the local newspaper for a cartoonist. The ad had been placed by a firm called the Kansas City Film Ad Company, which produced short cartoons for local businesses.

Walt had never lost his interest in cartooning, and he and Ub had recently become interested in the filmed cartoons that were appearing in Kansas City theaters. Ub was particularly impressed with a film about a dinosaur made by newspaper cartoonist Winsor McCay. The dinosaur, Ub told Walt excitedly, was a real character with a personality all its own! Ub didn't know it, but Gertie the Dinosaur was the first cartoon character to which an artist had given a personality. Most early cartoons were simply animated drawings of funny situations.

Walt tried to catch the cartoon at the theater, but the feature had changed and the cartoon along with it.

The opening at Kansas City Film Ad Company seemed like just what Walt and Ub had been looking for to learn the film cartoon business. They decided that Walt would apply for the job, using his sales skills to convince the Kansas City Film Ad Company that they needed two cartoonists, not one. But it didn't work out quite the way the two had imagined. The Kansas City Film Ad Company offered the job to Walt alone.

"Forty dollars a week!" Walt told Ub.

The two young men looked at each other, amazed. Forty dollars a week was more money than they had ever dreamed of earning! Ub told Walt that he must take the job; Ub would carry on with Iwerks-Disney alone. Walt agreed, relieved that Ub was not upset. He turned all the assets of the little company over to Ub and the two shook hands on the deal.

At his new firm, Walt threw himself into learning the essentials of *animation*, as film cartooning is called. Kansas

City Film Ad Company made short cartoons for local businesses, which paid movie theater owners to run them in between feature films. To produce a cartoon, the artists drew figures, then cut them out and fixed them to a drawing board. The arms and legs of the figures were jointed and could be placed in different positions.

The cameraman moved the figure's limbs into a position, photographed it, then moved the limbs to a slightly different position and photographed it again. The same process was repeated over and over, until the cameraman had hundreds of photographs, each one showing a slight change of position. When the photographs were combined on a strip of film, the figure looked as though it was moving, although in a rather jerky, unnatural way.

Fascinated with his new job, Walt tried to find out all he could about animation. He visited the Kansas City Public Library to read up on the subject. There he read about Winsor McCay, creator of Gertie the Dinosaur, and other early animators. He quickly realized that the methods used at his new firm were old-fashioned. In New York City, the animation center of the world at that time, animators *drew* the figures on plastic material called celluloid. The celluloid was transparent, so a number of figures could be placed over the same background.

Drawing made for a smoother, more realistic motion. Walt began drawing his figures, and his employers were pleased with the results. But they still fell short of Walt's expectations.

The person he needed to help him make the large number of really good drawings he needed for superior animation,

Winsor McCay's Gertie the Dinosaur was the first cartoon character with personality. Walt and Ub remembered her when they made their first cartoons. —MUSEUM OF MODERN ART/FILM STILLS ARCHIVES

Walt realized, was the talented Ub Iwerks. Ub, Walt knew, was having trouble with Iwerks-Disney. Unlike Walt, Ub was a poor salesman, and in Walt's absence his business had dwindled to almost nothing. Walt persuaded Kansas City Film Ad Company to hire Ub, and soon the two young men were working together again.

Walt would do the rough sketches for a cartoon idea and give them to Ub, who would turn out a pile of excellent drawings in an incredibly short time.

In spite of his skills, Ub remained the same shy, inarticulate, serious young man he had been when Walt first met him. He was extremely nervous around young women. Ub's personality made him a natural foil for confident Walt's practical jokes. At Kansas City Film Ad Company, Walt would send Ub postcards signed with girls' names, lock him in the washroom so that he had to hammer on the door to get out, and smuggle animals into his desk and locker. Ub never complained.

During the first months that Walt was with his new employer, Roy had continued trying to find a cartoonist's job for his younger brother on one of the Kansas City newspapers. Roy worked in a bank and he had customers who advertised with the newspapers. Roy showed the customers Walt's cartoons. Walt had been at Kansas City Film Ad Company only a short time when he received a job offer he would have jumped at before. The *Kansas City Star's* morning paper needed a cartoonist. Was Walt interested?

Walt turned them down. "They had their chance," he told Roy.

Roy didn't argue with Walt. From the tone of Walt's

voice, Roy understood that he had found what he wanted to do.

Walt had become friendly with the cameraman at Kansas City Film Ad Company, who showed Walt how he photographed figures to make them look as though they were moving. After a while he let Walt do some of the camera work himself. Now that he could operate the camera, Walt had an idea. Why not film his own cartoons?

At this time, Roy and Walt were both still living at the old family home at 3028 Bellefontaine Avenue with their brother Hubert and his wife. Walt set up a studio in the garage of the Bellefontaine home and borrowed a camera from his employer. After working all day at Kansas City Film Ad Company, he and Ub would go into the little garage studio and work on their own cartoons. The first one they did was inspired by a popular cartoon series, *Out of the Inkwell*, by Max Fleisher. A satire on the poor condition of Kansas City streets, it showed vehicles literally shaking apart as they negotiated a pothole-filled street.

Walt sold the film to a man named Milton Feld, who managed a chain of theaters called the Newman Theaters. Feld suggested other ideas for cartoons, and soon these little shorts, called Laugh-o-Grams, were appearing in Kansas City theaters. They became very popular and Walt found himself something of a local celebrity. His employers admired the Laugh-o-Grams but turned Walt down when the young employee suggested that Kansas City Film Ad do cartoons of its own.

But they did raise Walt's salary to a sum he had hardly dreamed of before: sixty dollars a week!

In 1920, the year Walt joined Kansas City Film Ad Company, Roy began having serious health problems. He had always been thin, but now he looked gaunt and pale. At night Walt heard him coughing in the room next to his. Later that year, Roy's doctors discovered that he had tuberculosis. It was a serious illness in 1920. There were no antibiotics, and patients were treated with complete bed rest, preferably in a dry, warm climate. Many tuberculosis patients died. Roy was a veteran of World War I, so he was assigned to a veterans' hospital in New Mexico.

Walt and Roy's fiancée, Edna Francis, saw Roy off at the Kansas City train station. Edna was in tears and Walt had a lump in his throat as they said good-bye.

"I'll always be ready when you need any help," said Roy to his brother.

Then he was gone. His parting gift to Walt had been a hundred dollars in cash and a year's rent paid in advance for Walt's room at 3028 Bellefontaine and the garage. Roy had always provided financial aid to Walt, but he was more than a source of cash and sound financial advice for his younger brother. Roy gave Walt emotional support. Walt missed his brother acutely. He began sending him Get Well cards almost every day, and Roy responded with frequent letters.

Walt stayed in the Bellefontaine house for another year. During part of this time, Elias and Flora lived there, too. The Chicago jelly factory had failed, and Elias was again looking for work. But Kansas City proved to have a poor job market for the aging Elias, and in 1921 he sold the house. Elias, Flora, Ruth, and Hubert all moved to Oregon, where Hubert had been transferred by the Post Office.

Once again, Walt saw family members off at the Kansas City railroad station. Afterward, he shifted his belongings to a rooming house and rented a small shop for his studio.

By now, Walt wanted to make longer cartoons like the ones he had seen in the movie houses. To turn out the large number of drawings for such cartoons, however, he would need more artists. He advertised in the newspaper for artists who wanted to learn how to make filmed cartoons. He couldn't pay them, he explained, but they would share in any future profits. Five young men signed up, most of them in their teens. Walt hired a young woman, too, who traced the drawings onto the celluloid and then inked and colored them. Walt never even considered hiring her as an artist. To him, artists were men, and inkers and painters, as they were called, were women.

The first cartoon the young group produced was *Little Red Riding Hood*. Walt was so pleased with it that he quit his job at Kansas City Film Ad Company. He raised fifteen thousand dollars from local businessmen and bought cameras, a projector, film, and all the other equipment needed to produce filmed cartoons. He acquired something else at this time that was even more valuable than equipment: the services of Ub Iwerks. Walt persuaded Ub to quit his job and join Laugh-o-Gram Films.

Soon the little work force, which included a salesman, had turned out seven different cartoons. Walt was delighted with them, but the New York distribution company with whom the Disney salesman had made a deal failed to pay the money it owed. Walt kept the new firm going by shooting footage for newsreels and making movies of babies for new parents, but soon his funds had disappeared. The employees began to leave. Ub Iwerks went back to Kansas City Film Ad Company.

Walt gave up his room and moved into his offices, where the rent had been paid in advance. One night a mouse appeared on his desk and Walt gave him a bit of food. After that he fed the mouse regularly. Since the offices had no bathtub or shower, Walt used the one at the nearby railroad station. As he walked through the station, he saw the passengers and was reminded of the family members to whom he had said good-bye in recent years, particularly Roy.

At this low point, Walt received a five-hundred-dollar check from a local dentist to make a cartoon about dental health. After finishing the project, he decided to risk the money that was left on one roll of the dice—a new cartoon. An appealing child named Virginia Davis had been a model for Kansas City Film Ad, and Walt decided to use her in a cartoon with a number of cartoon animals.

The cartoon would be a twist on the popular *Out of the Inkwell* series, in which cartoon figures popped out of a cartoonist's inkwell and performed in front of live backgrounds. Walt's idea was to make a cartoon background for a live actress—Virginia Davis. He could obtain this effect, he knew, by photographing Virginia against a white background and then making the drawings on white backgrounds. In the printing process, both films would be put together.

He fired off a letter describing the project to some of his New York contacts, including Margaret Winkler, who distributed *Out of the Inkwell*. Miss Winkler sent back an encouraging letter, enough for Walt to plunge into production. Ub and some of the other animators had been hired back to make the dental health movie, and Walt put them to work drawing the cartoon animals for his new film, which he had named *Alice's Wonderland*. But by the time he had finished it, his money was almost gone.

When Roy received a letter describing Walt's money woes, the sick man responded with a blank check and instructions to fill it out for any sum up to thirty dollars. Walt promptly filled it out for thirty dollars and kept the project going awhile longer. But soon he was completely out of funds. He sent another letter to Roy, who had been moved to a veterans' hospital in Los Angeles.

"I don't think you can do any more for it," Roy wrote back.

Walt declared bankrupcy in 1923. His creditors allowed him to keep the footage that had been made of the *Alice* film and his camera. Before he left the office, he took the mouse he had been feeding to a woods and released it. By shooting newsreel footage, he managed to pay off most of his debts, although Ub got less than half of the money Walt owed him.

By now Walt was desperately tired of struggling to make cartoons. He wanted to leave Kansas City and go, not to New York, the capital of the cartoon-making industry, but to the West Coast. Roy was there, and in Hollywood, Walt thought, he could become a director of *live-action* comedy films, or films of real actors, like the ones in which his idol Charlie Chaplin starred.

As for cartoons, Walt was ready to let others make them.

In July of 1923, Walt used the last of his money to buy a first-class one-way ticket to Los Angeles. Edna and Ub came down to the railroad station to see him off. Walt wore a checked jacket, blue pants, and a bright red bow tie. He carried a small suitcase holding only two spare shirts and one spare set of underwear—all the clothes he had left. In his wallet was fifty dollars.

Everyone's eyes were wet as he waved goodbye from the train.

DAVID C. WERNER, *Managing Director*

WEEK BEGINNING SUNDAY, NOVEMBER 25th, 1928

Continuous Performance Noon to Midnight

De Luxe Performances at 2:00—4:00—7:40—9:40

1. "STEAMBOAT WILLIE"
   The FIRST animated cartoon with SOUND

2. COLONY TOPICS
   Selected Pictorial News of the World

3. WILLIAM Le BARON presents
   The FBO Special TALKING and SOUND Picture

"Gang War" (c. 1928)

with

Flowers	OLIVE BORDEN
Clyde	JACK PICKFORD
Blackjack	EDDIE GRIBBON
Mike Luego	WALTER LONG

GALA OPENING WEEK

BENNY RUBIN	JIMMY CARR
the inimitable	and his Famous
"Master of Ceremonies"	Silver Slipper Orchestra
returns to Broadway after a	as the original
tremendously successful engage-	
ment in California	*"Doctor of Melody"*

presenting

The Ultimate in Stage Presentations

featuring

BEE JACKSON

the creator of the Charleston in a NEW DANCE CREATION

The program distributed to patrons of the Colony Theater for the week of November 25, 1928. *Steamboat Willie*, the first cartoon with sound, is listed first, because it opened the program.—BILLY ROSE THEATRE COLLECTION, NEW YORK PUBLIC LIBRARY

Chapter Three

Walt had another relative in the Los Angeles area, too—
Robert Disney, his father's brother. Uncle Robert, who was
retired, let Walt use a room in his house. Roy was in the
Satelle Veterans Hospital, a long trolley ride from Uncle
Robert's house, and Walt made the trip a number of times
in the next few weeks. It had been three years since he had
seen Roy, and they had many things to talk about.

Walt also looked for a job as a director. He was particularly interested in directing comedy films like the ones in
which Charlie Chaplin appeared. But when he applied to
United Artists, Chaplin's studio, and to other studios with
comedy stars, no one was interested in an inexperienced
young man from the Midwest. Walt never even caught a
glimpse of Chaplin, although he lingered outside United
Artists' gate for hours.

But when his uncle and aunt treated him to brunch at
a well-known restaurant one Sunday, the Disneys were seated
right next to Chaplin's table! Walt talked about the event
for years.

After Walt had been living with his uncle and aunt for
a month or so, his uncle asked him for five dollars a month
for rent for his room. Walt had no money. There was only
one thing to do, he decided: return to making cartoons. He
still had the print of *Alice*. Perhaps, he thought, Margaret
Winkler, the New York film distributor who had once been
interested in the film, hadn't forgotten it. He sent her a
copy of the film and a letter explaining that he had relocated
in Los Angeles.

"I am taking with me a select number of my former staff
and will in a very short time be producing at regular inter-

vals," he wrote, even though he had no staff, no studio, and no equipment except his camera.

In a short time, a telegram arrived from Miss Winkler. Walt ripped it open in front of his uncle and aunt and let out a shout. The telegram offered Walt fifteen hundred dollars for each completed Alice film—provided the same child actress played Alice. Walt raced out of the house without informing his uncle and aunt what the telegram said. He boarded the trolley car for the veterans' hospital.

Tuberculosis patients spent much of their time resting in those days, and Roy and the other patients in his ward were sleeping when Walt arrived. Walt woke his brother up and shoved the telegram in front of him. The two brothers discussed the contract Miss Winkler proposed in whispers. Roy, as usual, looked at the financial picture. Could Walt deliver the Alice films for fifteen hundred dollars apiece?

"For half of that," cried Walt, his voice rising. But only, he added, if Roy joined him in the venture. "I need your help, Roy. You've got to get out of here and join me!"

Roy was silent while Walt outlined the reasons why he should join his brother. Finally, the patient in the next bed spoke up. "Say yes, and then we can all get back to sleep!"

The next morning, Roy signed himself out of the hospital.

Uncle Robert loaned his two nephews five hundred dollars and this, added to Roy's savings, enabled Walt and Roy to buy the equipment they needed to produce the six films. By the time Virginia Davis arrived from Kansas City to play Alice, they were working out of a small building a few doors away from Uncle Robert's house.

After the first six Alice films were produced, Disney Brothers

Productions, as the new firm was called, got a contract for more. Ub Iwerks joined them in 1924. He received ten dollars less a month than he had been making at Kansas City Film Ad Company, but he was given a twenty-percent interest in Disney Brothers Productions. Now Walt no longer had to draw. He spent his time developing stories and funny situations for Alice.

The Alice films got good reviews, particularly after Ub joined the staff, but they made little money for the Disneys. Margaret Winkler had married Charles Mintz, who took over her business. He was a slow payer. Walt wrote to Mintz again and again, pleading for money Mintz owed them. At one point the two brothers were so desperate that they borrowed $25 from Edna Francis, Roy's fiancée in Kansas City, and $275 from Carl Stallings, a Kansas City organist.

To save money, Walt and Roy shared a one-room apartment. Roy did the cooking. He was a poor cook, though, and Walt, who liked food, often complained. One night, after Walt complained yet again, Roy dumped a plate full of stew on his brother. The next day, Roy telegraphed Edna Francis. Roy and Edna were married in 1925 at Uncle Robert's home, with Walt as best man.

Walt was now alone in his rented room. Unable to cook and unwilling to clean, he found life far from comfortable.

By now Disney Brothers Productions had a handful of employees, including two young women inkers. One of them was Lillian Bounds. Walt had bought a secondhand car, a popular model called the Moon, and he began taking Lillian for rides. He had often said that he would not get married until he was twenty-five and had ten thousand dollars in the bank, but he fell short of both goals. On July 13, 1925, when Walt was twenty-three years old and had very little in the bank, he and Lilly, as Walt called her, were married in her home town in Idaho.

A few months later, Disney Brothers Productions moved to a one-story building they had erected on a lot on Hyperion Avenue, a few miles from downtown Los Angeles. After the move, the firm was called the Walt Disney Studio. The name of one single person, Walt reasoned, would have more "box office appeal," and besides, he was in charge. Roy did not object. He seemed content to let his younger brother have the spotlight while he handled the finances behind the scenes.

By 1926, Charles Mintz was having trouble selling Alice. When Margaret Winkler Mintz visited the new Hyperion Avenue studio, she suggested to Walt that he try something new: a cartoon starring a rabbit. Universal Pictures, one of Hollywood's big studios, was looking for a rabbit series. Walt immediately sat down at a drawing board and sketched a rabbit. Within days, Universal approved the sketches for the rabbit, who was named Oswald.

Ub turned Walt's sketches into a cartoon with a plump, elderly rabbit. Universal hated it.

At first Walt and Ub were stunned by Universal's criticism. But as Walt mulled it over, he realized that it was at least partly deserved. Back in Kansas City, he and Ub had dreamed of creating a cartoon animal with a strong personality. But their Oswald had little personality. Walt and Ub discussed the problem and then Ub went back to the drawing board. He came up with a younger, slimmer Oswald with a personality that leaped right off the screen.

Oswald looked a lot like a long-eared Mickey Mouse. —*BEFORE MICKEY*, MIT PRESS

The critics loved the new Oswald. So did the public. And so did Universal and Charles Mintz. For the first time, Mintz paid on time. With a little money in the bank, Walt and Roy were able to hire more animators. They also bought adjoining lots near the studio and put up two identical small houses. Walt was in high spirits as he and Lillian took the train to New York early in 1928 to sign a new Oswald contract. He was going to ask for more money and he was sure he would get it.

But Mintz offered Walt less money, not more. Then Mintz dropped a bombshell. If the Disneys didn't accept his offer, he threatened, he would take their animators. Most of them had secretly signed contracts with him already. Universal, he reminded Walt, owned Oswald and was prepared to produce the cartoon without Walt. Stunned, Walt hurried back to his hotel and called Roy. Soon Roy telephoned back with the bad news. All but three of the fourteen animators had signed contracts with Mintz. Ub was one of the exceptions.

Mintz made Walt an offer. He was prepared to pay all the expenses of making Oswald cartoons. All Walt had to do was sign a contract making Mintz and Universal partners in the Walt Disney Studio.

Walt appealed to Universal, but the big studio backed up Mintz. Walt was bitter. Mintz and Universal wanted to take over his studio! "Never again will I work for somebody else," he told Lilly. As he walked the crowded streets of New York City, he came to a decision. Without telling Roy, Walt made a last visit to Mintz's office. He flung a badge with the likeness of Oswald onto Mintz's big desk.

"He's all yours!" shouted Walt.

"How are you going to get by without Oswald?" Mintz wanted to know.

"Don't worry," said Walt, "there are plenty more characters where he came from."

Walt and Lilly boarded the westbound train. It was a three-day trip, and Walt spent much of his time at his drawing board, doodling. Somehow, he began thinking of the mouse family with whom he had shared his office in those lonely days in Kansas City. A mouse. Big ears, a pointed snout, button eyes. He passed the sketches over to Lilly and told her he would like to call the new character Mortimer.

Lilly didn't like the name. "Mickey," she said. "Mickey Mouse."

Roy was appalled by the news that Walt had rejected Mintz's offer, even when Walt told him he had already found a new character. He needed something on *film* to sell the idea, Roy pointed out. Walt wasted no time. He showed his sketches to Ub, who liked the name Mickey, too. He added that the mouse looked like Walt. Actually, the mouse looked very much like Oswald, except that Mickey had large round mouse ears while Oswald had long floppy rabbit ears. The two animals were obviously closely related.

Walt and Ub spent many hours discussing Mickey's personality. He would be gallant, mischievous, resourceful, and wistful, they decided. Walt was later to say that Mickey Mouse's personality owed much to Charlie Chaplin. The animators who had signed up with Mintz were still at the studio, drawing the last Oswald cartoons. Fearing that they would find out about Mickey, Walt arranged for Ub to work in the garage of his new house. Standing in front of Ub's drawing board, Walt acted out all the scenes in which Mickey appeared.

Ub had always been a speedy worker, and to produce Mickey he turned out six hundred drawings a day. Lillian and Edna inked and colored the drawings onto celluloid. After the studio closed for the day, Walt photographed the celluloids.

On May 15, 1928, the first Mickey Mouse cartoon was previewed at a Hollywood movie house. The audience received it without much interest. Movie executives and distributors who saw it were lukewarm, too. Walt was so enthusiastic about Mickey, though, that he put another Mickey cartoon into production. It aroused no more enthusiasm than the first one. Walt was frustrated. He was convinced that the Mickey cartoons were the best thing he had done and, in fact, the best filmed cartoons *anyone* had done.

But how could he sell them?

A few months before the first Mickey Mouse cartoon was previewed, the movie industry had been changed forever by a single film. It was *The Jazz Singer*, the first feature film with sound. *The Jazz Singer* was a tremendous success, and soon every producer in Hollywood was trying to make sound movies. The sound movie, Walt realized, was the movie of the future. What Mickey Mouse needed was sound. He would make a third Mickey Mouse cartoon with music, sound effects—and Mickey's voice!

First, though, he had to figure out how to add sound to a cartoon. Luckily, one of the new animators the Walt

Disney Studio had hired was Wilfred Jackson, a young man with a background in music. At Jackson's suggestion, a metronome was set up next to the film projector. While the latest Mickey cartoon, known as *Steamboat Willie*, was projected on the screen, Jackson played tunes on his harmonica and Walt calculated how many frames of cartoon would be needed to match the music. Then Ub used Disney's calculations to make his drawings.

Later Walt added other sound effects and a high-pitched version of his own voice for Mickey's squeaky voice. Carl Stallings, the Kansas City organist who had made a crucial loan to the Disney brothers, composed a score for the film.

Now Walt had to have the score recorded on his films. This was a job for experts, so six months after he had thrown his Oswald badge at Charles Mintz, Walt found himself back in New York City. RCA had pioneered the sound-on-film system and was generally believed to have the best system. RCA, Walt thought, was the system for him. But when he saw an old silent cartoon to which RCA had added sound, he was so upset by the poor sound quality that he decided to look elsewhere.

He heard about a new firm, Cinephone, which claimed to be able to record sound on film. Pat Powers, who headed Cinephone, had actually bribed engineers at RCA to build him a recording system like that of RCA. But Walt didn't know that then. All he knew was that Powers had powerful friends and was much more pleasant to deal with than Charles Mintz. Putting his arm around Walt's shoulder, Powers told him that Cinephone would solve his sound problems. Walt agreed to pay his fee of one thousand dollars, plus a royalty on the Mickey cartoons. Walt Disney Studio would also pay for the orchestra.

The first suspicion Walt had that the sound recording was not going to go smoothly came when he met with the orchestra conductor. The conductor refused to use the simple system of white marks on the film that Walt had set up to make sure the music kept pace with the film. Walt, he said, should leave the conducting to the conductor. When the recording session got under way, though, the conductor kept ending up with pages of music and sound effects left over after the cartoon came to an end.

After the orchestra members had gone to lunch, the conductor turned to Walt and told him he would try the system he had suggested.

The new recording session, Walt figured, would cost another twelve hundred dollars. He telephoned Roy. There wasn't enough money in the bank to cover the second session, so Roy sold the new Moon automobile Walt had bought to replace his secondhand one. At the second session, the conductor followed the white marks on the film, and at the end of a long, tiring day, the seven-minute cartoon had sound. When Walt ran it through for the first time with sound, he knew he had been right: without sound, *Steamboat Willie* was a good cartoon, but with it, the cartoon was terrific.

Since Walt no longer had a film distributor, he made an arrangement with Pat Powers to show the cartoon to distributors in the New York City area. But Mickey Mouse with sound got the same treatment in New York that the silent Mickey had in Los Angeles. Many distributors viewed the film, and most of them laughed a lot. But no one wanted to distribute it. One day, while Walt was standing in the lobby of a theater, listening to the distributors' comments, a man came up to him.

Introducing himself as Harry Reichenbach, the man offered to show *Steamboat Willie* at New York's Colony Theater, which he managed. He would pay Walt five hundred dollars per week.

The cartoon opened on November 18, 1928, and after that nothing was quite the same for the Walt Disney Studio. This time Mickey was an immediate hit—with the critics, with the public, and with the distributors. One of them was Charles Mintz. Mintz offered Walt a deal: Universal, which Mintz represented, would give Walt all the financial backing he needed, as well as a generous share of the profits if he would bring Mickey Mouse to Universal. Universal, of course, would then control Mickey.

Walt listened, tempted. He and Roy would be rich if they took the offer. He would never have to sell his automobile again to pay a bill.

But Universal would control his creation—Mickey.

Walt didn't even discuss the offer with Roy. He knew he could never accept anyone controlling one of his creations again. "No," he said.

Pat Powers had also attended the meeting. As they walked back to Disney's hotel, the famous Algonquin on West Forty-fourth Street, Powers offered him another deal. He would advance Walt the money to make Mickey cartoons and pay salesmen to sell them. In return, he asked for only 10 percent of the gross—the amount the films would make before expenses were deducted. To Walt, who was weary of deals and the slippery personalities of the film world, Powers's offer was very appealing. He signed a one-year contract without checking with Roy.

Before he left New York, Walt went back to the Colony to see *Steamboat Willie* one more time. As people laughed at the antics of Mickey, Minnie, and their companions, tears began to roll down Walt's cheeks.

Back in Los Angeles, Roy wasn't nearly as pleased with Walt's contract with Powers as Walt was. Roy had heard some unpleasant rumors about Powers. Walt brushed Roy's fears aside. Now that Powers was ready to sell Mickey Mouse cartoons, Walt Disney Studio had to get to work. Walt dreamed up story ideas while Ub carried them out. Ub had the assistance of other animators, but he was chiefly responsible for the drawings of Mickey.

Some time before, Walt had begun a new policy. When Ub or another animator had completed enough rough drawings, Walt had them photographed. Then the drawings were screened so that Walt could get some idea of what the finished cartoon would look like. Only when he was satisfied did he allow the cartoonists to do the finished artwork. Adding this extra step was time-consuming and expensive, but it produced better cartoons.

All during 1929, Walt Disney Studio fairly churned with activity. Walt and Ub often worked far into the night. Oddly enough, however, this frantic activity produced very little money. Pat Powers was selling cartoons, but he sent the Disneys only small sums. Expenses took most of the money, he explained. Walt, tired and nervous, began snapping at

Ub. Sometimes he would literally tear Ub's sketches off the drawing board and throw them across the room. They were not what he wanted, he would shout.

Ub never said anything when Walt was in one of his rages.

By the end of 1929, the work of Walt and Ub had made Mickey Mouse famous. Theaters began putting Mickey Mouse's name on the marquee, along with the name of the feature. Newspaper cartoonists used the little animal in their cartoons. Magazine reporters wrote about him. King Features approached Walt Disney Studio with an idea for a Mickey Mouse comic strip, and Ub turned out the first few strips.

Walt, his employees noticed, seemed to take a personal interest in Mickey. When a future cartoon was being discussed, Walt often said "Mickey wouldn't do that," as if he had some inner knowledge of the mouse's thought processes. He frequently acted out some piece of action in which the mouse was engaged for the benefit of the animators. More and more, drawings of Mickey resembled Walt's facial expressions and movements. And Walt kept on using his own voice for Mickey. At the studio, Walt *was* Mickey Mouse.

And from the way he responded to Mickey, it was obvious that Walt identified with Mickey, too. Mickey was his alter ego.

During this period, Elias and Flora, together with Ruth, visited Walt and Roy in Los Angeles. By now, the rift that had existed between Walt and Roy and their father had been healed. The two sons conducted their parents and sister

Walt, second from left, wears his usual sweater at a work session in 1930. The others, left to right, are Bert Lewis, Bert Gillett, and Ted Sears.—MARK WANAMAKER, BISON ARCHIVES

proudly through the Hyperion Avenue studio, showing them how Mickey Mouse was created. At one point, Ruth remembers, Walt said, "I'm going to make the name of Disney famous throughout the world!"

For every moment of euphoria like this, though, Walt had many moments of despair. Powers was still sending the Disney brothers almost no money. By the end of the one-year contract, Walt had joined Roy in his distrust of Powers. Walt took the train back to New York to confront Powers in person. Powers, like Mintz, dropped a bombshell. If Walt Disney Studio didn't sign another contract with him, they would never see their money. It would cost them too much to fight him in the courts to get it. What's more, he added, he had signed a contract with Ub Iwerks.

Ub had indeed resigned. He had told Roy that he couldn't stand the tension at the studio. To Walt, the scenario was all too familiar. Once again, people were letting him down. Once again, he was being cheated. But this time it was worse, because Ub was one of the people involved. Ub, the man with whom he had started out on his animation career! The man who had helped him put Mickey Mouse on the screen. The man who understood what he wanted to do almost as well as he understood it himself. And the man who was his oldest and closest friend.

Stalling for time, Walt told Powers he needed money right away. Powers gave him a check for $5,000, which Walt immediately dispatched to the studio to meet some pressing bills. After a number of phone conferences, Walt and Roy came to a reluctant decision. Although Roy figured that Powers owed them about $150,000, they would not fight him in court. They would let him keep the money he owed them.

When Walt returned to Los Angeles, the Disney brothers signed a contract with Columbia Pictures to finance and distribute their films. Columbia loaned them the money to pay Powers for the rights to cartoons he had already distributed. As for Ub, the brothers paid him what his twenty-percent share of the Walt Disney Studio was then worth—less than three thousand dollars. Ub began working for Powers. Later he would have his own studio.

In 1930, Roy and his wife Edna had a son, whom they named Roy Edward. Walt and Lilly wanted a baby, too, but Lilly could not become pregnant.

At the studio, Walt was even more critical and demanding and preoccupied than he had been before. He often walked right past studio employees without even seeing them. He worked some sixteen hours a day, returning to the studio after dinner and staying there until the early hours of the morning. The quality of the cartoons kept improving and Mickey Mouse's fame grew. But at the Walt Disney Studio, money remained short. Walt was spending so much on each cartoon that it barely paid for the next one.

Walt began to have trouble sleeping and took sleeping pills. One day in 1931, Lilly was unable to wake him.

Walt's doctors prescribed a long trip for some rest and relaxation. He and Lilly set out for Washington, D.C. As he watched the scenery flash by the train windows, Walt must have felt confused. At the age of thirty, he had achieved fame beyond his wildest dreams. He was doing just what he had always wanted to do. And he was miserable.

The old Hyperion Avenue studio.—MARK WANAMAKER, BISON
ARCHIVES

Chapter Four

Walt and Lilly took a long cruise after seeing the sights in Washington. By the time he returned to the Hyperion Avenue studio two months later, Walt was feeling much better. While he had been away, Roy had found a new distributor, United Artists. United Artists gave Walt Disney Productions, as the firm was now called, much more favorable terms than had Columbia.

Walt was pleased, and not just about the terms. United Artists was the studio of Charlie Chaplin, the comic he admired more than any other.

One of the first projects on which Walt was involved under the new contract with United Artists was a cartoon called *Flowers and Trees*, which didn't feature Mickey Mouse. As far back as 1929, Walt had begun to make short films without Mickey. He believed that to survive in the fickle film industry, where tastes changed rapidly, he had to make a variety of films. His 1929 film, *The Skeleton Dance*, was hard to sell.

"MORE MICE," Pat Powers had telegraphed Walt.

But Walt convinced a Los Angeles theater owner to show the film, and people liked it. After that, Walt began to make other cartoons without Mickey, calling each one a Silly Symphony. When he saw the complete version of *Flowers and Trees*, however, he had doubts. The film was a fanciful story about two trees that fall in love. It was well-drawn, but in Walt's opinion it lacked interest.

By 1932, a firm called Technicolor had developed a method of using color in animated films. Until this time, all movies, including Disney cartoons, were in black and white. Walt saw a demonstration of Technicolor's new process and immediately saw its advantages for cartoons, just as he had seen the advantages of sound. He made a decision. They would refilm *Flowers and Trees* in color. It would be the first color cartoon!

Roy was horrified. Filming the cartoon in color would multiply its costs by two-thirds, he pointed out. Besides, he had learned that Ub Iwerks was going to ask Technicolor to film one of his cartoons, so Walt's film would not be unique. When he heard this news, Walt went to Technicolor and asked them to give him exclusive rights to their process for two years.

Technicolor agreed, and *Flowers and Trees* became the first color cartoon. In 1932, it won an Academy Award. The same year, Walt won another award for developing Mickey Mouse.

Mickey was still the top star of Walt Disney Productions in 1932, but soon the studio had other popular cartoon characters. Goofy and Pluto first appeared in the early 1930s. Donald Duck came along in 1934. At first Donald was just one animal character among others. What he needed, Walt thought, was the right voice. One day Walt was listening to a radio show devoted to amateur talent. A contestant named Clarence Nash quacked into the mike, pretending he was a duck.

Donald Duck! thought Walt.

Nash, a teacher, dubbed his voice for Donald, and another cartoon star was born. Nash joined the studio full-time just to make Donald Duck cartoons.

To animate Mickey and all the other cartoon characters, more and more artists were hired. By 1934, there were two hundred employees at Walt Disney Productions, about half of them artists. Walt broke down the artists' duties into a kind of artistic assembly line. Some worked on the story, some worked on the backgrounds, some did the more important animation, some did what was called in-between work—the less important animation. And a few artists concentrated on art that Walt hoped would simply inspire the other artists.

Even the animators themselves had specialties. Some proved better at drawing certain characters, so that character became "their" character. In 1933, for instance, Walt drew a picture of Porker, the pig he remembered from Marceline, and circulated it among the artists along with a script for a version of the *Three Little Pigs*. A new artist, Fred Moore, produced drawings of a pig that looked like Porker. Walt liked the sketches so much that he gave Moore the job of drawing the pigs for the cartoon. It won another Academy Award for Walt in 1933.

Walt would usually drop into the office of each of his major artists every day. He would listen to the story editors summarize their work in progress, check the work of the background artists, and view the animators' rough drawings in the "sweatbox," as the animators' screening room was known. Shamus Culhane, one of the animators who worked at the studio in the early years, remembers that Walt was amazingly good at putting his finger on any problem during these daily visits.

To Culhane, one of the major differences between the Disney studio and other cartoon studios in the mid-1930s was that at Disney, the animators were trying to develop

Walt (left) and Roy with an early Oscar.—MARK WANAMAKER,
BISON ARCHIVES

cartoons that stressed character and plot, not just slapstick comedy. All the early cartoons, even Walt's, had been simply a series of gags. By 1936, though, Disney was turning out cartoons like *The Country Cousin*, which had a strong plot and two leading characters who really "acted." This cartoon won an Academy Award.

Even when his animators were turning out work superior to that of anyone in the field, Walt didn't give them screen credits for their work. He once explained why to a young animator who had just joined the staff. "What we're selling here is the name Walt Disney," Walt told the artist. "If you can swallow that and always remember it, you'll be happy here. But if you've got any ideas about seeing your name up there, it's best for you to leave right away."

Most of the artists accepted Walt's arguments. But some didn't. Later, their dissatisfaction would lead to problems.

As the public took the Disney cartoon characters to their hearts, manufacturers and other businessmen began using them to sell everything from bars of soap to handkerchiefs. At first Walt Disney Productions made no charge for the use of their characters, figuring that it was good advertising. By the early 1930s, however, they charged a small fee, which many manufacturers simply ignored.

In 1932, Herman "Kay" Kamen, a Kansas City advertising executive, made the Disneys an offer. He would handle all the details of selling the Disney characters and guarantee them the first fifty thousand dollars a year. Any further proceeds would be split 50-50. All the merchandise that carried the Disney characters, Kamen stressed, would be "quality" merchandise. Walt and Roy accepted. Kamen was soon putting $2.5 million into the Disney account every year.

Thanks to Kamen's merchandising abilities and the new contract with United Artists, money began to roll into Walt Disney Productions. Walt took up a very expensive sport, polo, and bought a dozen polo ponies. He encouraged Lilly to buy clothes from well-known designers. And when she at last became pregnant in 1933, Walt bought a big new house—with a swimming pool. Diane Disney was born on December 18, 1933.

The Disneys were at last successful. But Walt, as usual, was looking for new challenges. He had been mulling over a different kind of animated film for some time. One reason was economics. His short cartoons were successful, but they could never make much money. Film rental was the major source of Disney revenue and rental costs were determined solely by running time. But Walt had another reason for wanting to make a longer film. It would give him a chance to develop more complex plots and greater realism.

In 1933, Walt established an art school right at the studio to teach the new animators, as well as the old ones, a new style of cartooning. What he wanted to achieve, Walt told the artists, was realism. Animals and people should move smoothly, like the actors in live-action films. The art school, which was run by the Chouinard Art Institute of Los Angeles, held classes in drawing animal and human models.

Walt called some of his animators together after the studio had closed one evening in 1934. He led the group to a stage used for sound production and had them take chairs. Then Walt began to tell them a story, just as he did when they were starting work on a new short cartoon. But this story was different. Once upon a time, he said, there was a beautiful young princess who had an evil stepmother.

It was the story of *Snow White and the Seven Dwarfs*, which Walt had seen in a live-action version long ago in Kansas City.

Walt was a superb storyteller, and the animators sat enthralled for several hours as he acted out the story, playing all the roles in turn. He was the wicked queen, he was Snow White, he was the huntsman the Queen orders to kill Snow White, he was the prince, and he was every one of the seven dwarfs. At the end of the story, when the prince's kiss awakens Snow White, most of the animators had tears in their eyes.

The film, Walt told the animators, would be their first full-length feature.

Not only would the new venture be the length of a live-action feature film, he explained, but it would have music. The *Three Little Pigs* had a song, "Who's Afraid of the Big Bad Wolf?" which became a hit and poured more money into the Disney bank account. The new cartoon feature would have a number of songs, as Walt saw it, all of them growing out of the action of the film itself, like the song in *Three Little Pigs*.

The animators were enthusiastic, but when Walt outlined the project for Roy, the moneyman demanded to know how much it would cost.

Walt, who had drawn up a preliminary budget, named the sum of half a million dollars, which the brothers had in the bank. Walt suggested, however, that they borrow the money, paying it back from the box office receipts. Eventually, he argued, long films would make much more money than short films. But Roy didn't accept Walt's logic. Why, he asked, couldn't they stay with their big success, Mickey Mouse?

Almost everyone else in the film community asked the same question. *Snow White* would not only be Walt Disney Productions' first cartoon feature, it would be the first cartoon feature produced by any studio. The common opinion of the day was that people would not watch a cartoon lasting an hour and a half, the usual length of feature films in the 1930s. Even Lilly questioned the wisdom of making a feature-length cartoon.

Walt was aware of the problems involved in a feature-length cartoon and he was prepared to overcome them. One problem was the unrealistic movement of cartoons. His art school, Walt hoped, would enable his animators to make Snow White and the other human characters move like real people. "Never best at one," he would say, meaning that the animators would do their best drawings only after many attempts.

Another problem was the lack of depth in cartoons. Since cartoons were simply drawings on clear celluloid laid over a background, they looked flat, like drawings.

Walt had a solution for this, too, although it was still under development. It was a towering device called the multiplane camera. In the multiplane camera, the various parts of a scene—background, foreground, and characters— are mounted on glass plates that are placed at different levels. The camera is mounted on top of a fourteen-foot-high platform, with the glass plates below it. The camera-man shoots down, moving the camera through the various levels to achieve an effect of depth.

Walt wasted no time getting *Snow White* into production. He installed a small group of artists next to his office and held the first of what were to be literally hundreds of story conferences. Everyone who ever worked with Walt Disney agrees that his greatest talent lay in his role as a story editor at these conferences. He could tell a story so that his listeners would see it as it would appear on the screen.

Although Walt was the most important element in the story conference, it was a democratic process, with directors and animators contributing ideas. The final decision, how-ever, always lay with Walt.

The storyboard, which later came to be used at almost all the Hollywood studios, was an outgrowth of the Disney story conferences. It started with animator Webb Smith, who pinned rough drawings to his office walls so he could keep track of the action. Walt liked the idea and had cork-board installed in all the animators' offices for ease in pin-ning up drawings. At story conferences, key drawings from the scene under discussion would be pinned up in sequence so that everyone could follow the action.

As the preparations for *Snow White* got under way, Walt realized that an animated feature running an hour and a half would require an enormous number of drawings. There were not enough artists at the studio to produce them. He needed three hundred artists, Walt told Don Graham, head of the Disney art school. Soon the studio on Hyperion Avenue was bursting with new talent—and bursting out of

Walt never forgot the screen version of Marguerite Clark's *Snow White*, which he saw as a boy in Kansas City.—Free Library of Philadelphia

the office space. New buildings were put up and others rented up and down the street.

On *Snow White*, Walt instituted what would become his standard procedure. Certain artists were used to make drawings of settings and characters. When Walt was satisfied, the characters and some of the sets were modeled in three dimensions. Animators and background artists used these preliminary drawings and models to produce the actual art seen in the film. For the character of Snow White herself, Walt chose drawings of a round-faced, dark-haired young girl who looked surprisingly like Marguerite Clark, star of the live-action movie he had seen so long ago.

Walt, as usual, worked harder than anyone. In 1935, he began having the same nervous symptoms he had had in 1931. Roy suggested the same treatment: a vacation. The League of Nations planned to present Walt with a medal for the development of Mickey Mouse, who was now known worldwide. Walt and Lilly went to Paris to accept it. When they returned, three months later, Walt had regained his emotional health. He brought back a number of European storybooks in which he had found suggestions for the background paintings for *Snow White*.

At the studio, the animation work was proceeding slowly, even with the help of the new artists. It's a fact of life in film-making that animated films take much longer to produce than live-action films. Ollie Johnson and Frank Thomas, two veteran Disney animators, once explained why. There are about 7,200 feet of film to be animated in a typical Disney film of 80 minutes. The average animator can turn out about 10 feet a week.

Walt and Lilly sailed to Europe in 1935 so Walt could receive a special medal for the creation of Mickey Mouse.—BILLY ROSE THEATRE COLLECTION, NEW YORK PUBLIC LIBRARY

At that rate, 10 men doing 10 feet a week would take 72 weeks to do 7,200 feet—if they didn't take vacation or sick leave. And then, of course, time is needed for research, scoring the music, and other time-consuming work.

Johnson and Thomas figured that it took a minimum of three years and six months to turn out the average animated feature. In *Snow White*, however, the animators faced problems they had never encountered before. After viewing the early sketches on film, Walt realized the animators had a problem translating human movement into drawings. So he hired live actors to play the leading characters and filmed key scenes with the actors in costume. The animators used stills from the films to guide them.

The young dancer who played Snow White for the Disney animators was Margery Belcher. Later, as Marge Champion, she became a part of the well-known movie dance team Gower and Champion.

Margery was the inspiration for how Snow White *moved*, but how would Snow White sound? She would have several songs to sing in the film. Walt had a girl's voice in mind— high, young, and pure. He didn't want to be influenced by the way the singers looked, so he had a system rigged up that brought the sound of the singer into his office from the sound stage. Singer after singer was tested, including Deanna Durbin, a well-known movie actress in the 1930s. But Walt wasn't satisfied.

Then, one day, he heard a voice that made him say, "Perfect!" It belonged to Andriana Caselotti, an amateur singer who had studied opera. She became Snow White's voice.

The cost of filming the live action, the new artists, the

new work space, and all the other expenses exhausted the half million dollars Walt had budgeted for the film before the animation was complete. Walt and Roy borrowed money from the Bank of America. Soon the new loan ran out as well. Word got around Hollywood that Walt was having trouble making the film. "Disney's folly," people whispered. Roy went back to Joseph Rosenberg, a director of the Bank of America. Rosenberg had heard the whispers. He could advance no more money until he saw footage from the incomplete film, he told Roy.

Reluctantly, Walt pieced together a film consisting of the completed footage, bridged by long expanses of rough drawings without animation. Rosenberg viewed the footage on a Saturday in the Disneys' private projection room. As the film rolled, Walt filled in the gaps in the dialogue and action, acting out all the characters. At the end, he stood beside the screen, recreating the final scene where the prince kisses Snow White as she lies in her coffin.

Walt paused dramatically, his eyes on his audience, which consisted of Rosenberg, Roy, and a number of the animators.

Snow White, Walt said, begins to wake up! The music swells, the birds sing, the dwarfs hug each other . . .

One of the animators noticed that Roy had tears running down his cheeks. But Rosenberg seemed unmoved. When the lights went on, he calmly shook Walt's hand. Walt and Roy conducted him back to his car, parked outside the screening room. Rosenberg got inside and looked out the open window at the Disney brothers. "That thing is going to make a hatful of money," he said.

Crowds waiting outside Radio City Music Hall in New York City to see *Snow White* in 1938.—RADIO CITY MUSIC HALL

They got the money.

But the money pressure still existed. *Snow White* had to be finished, and finished soon. All through 1936 and early 1937, the animators and other artists worked long hours. Shamus Culhane remembers working Saturdays and Sundays. There was no overtime pay, and even the top animators received rather modest salaries—about one hundred dollars a week. But no one complained. Everyone was convinced that they were working on a breakthrough film.

While the work on *Snow White* was at its height, Walt and Lilly decided to adopt a baby. Their daughter Diane was now three, and Lilly, who was in her mid-thirties, had only had one pregnancy. She and Walt wanted another child, but in the 1930s there were few ways for physicians to help couples with fertility problems conceive a child. A little baby named Sharon joined the family in 1936.

As *Snow White* was being completed, the Disneys acquired a new distributor, RKO. They split with United Artists because UA wanted the brothers to give them the "television rights" to their films, and Walt didn't want to part with them, even though *television* was an unfamiliar word in 1937. There were no home sets, only experimental models. Walt declared he did not know what television was and he wasn't going to sign away anything he didn't understand.

Finally, late in 1937, *Snow White and the Seven Dwarfs* was complete. Its eighty-three minutes of running time required over two million finished drawings. The multiplane camera, which was still under development, could be used for only part of the footage, but it added dramatic effects to some scenes. Walt had promised the film to Radio City Music Hall in New York City for the Christmas season, but he wanted to hold the first public showing of the film closer to home.

On December 21, 1937, the world premiere of *Snow White and the Seven Dwarfs*—Walt always insisted on the full title—was held at the Cathay Circle Theater in Hollywood. The whispers now were that the film would be a hit. *Time* magazine had just done a cover story on Walt. A big crowd, including top stars and film-makers, was on hand at the premiere. At the end of the film, the entire audience rose to their feet and cheered. Walt went up on stage to accept their applause.

That night, the Disney animators went home with the knowledge, Shamus Culhane writes, that "we had worked on one of the greatest films in the history of motion pictures."

They liked the film just as much at Radio City Music Hall as they had in Hollywood. It broke all attendance records for its five-week run, and the reviews from the New York critics, usually a hard-to-please group, were sensational. After that, the film played all over the United States to huge audiences. Within six months, the Disneys had paid off their loans to the Bank of America. The film earned over $8 million in its first release, a record sum that was not surpassed by any film for a number of years.

The money enabled Walt Disney Productions to buy the land for a new studio in nearby Burbank. Fifty-five acres were purchased to make sure the studio had plenty of room for expansion.

Walt receives seven little Oscars and one big one for *Snow White* from child actress Shirley Temple.—ACADEMY OF MOTION PICTURE ARTS AND SCIENCES

Snow White and the Seven Dwarfs won the Academy Award for the best picture of 1937. Walt had received Academy Awards for cartoons, but this one was different. This was for a feature film. Shirley Temple, the famous child star of the 1930s, made the presentation. Shirley, who was ten, handed Walt not one Oscar but eight—one big one and seven little ones for the seven dwarfs. "Don't be nervous, Mr. Disney," she said, noticing Walt's shaking hands and perspiring face.

Walt smiled, clutching his Oscars. Disney's folly had become Disney's triumph.

Yes, Walt could draw. Here he draws Mickey for a young admirer at Greenfield Village near Detroit, Michigan, in 1940.—FROM THE COLLECTIONS OF HENRY FORD MUSEUM & GREENFIELD VILLAGE

Chapter Five

While *Snow White* was being made, Elias and Flora Disney were still living in Portland, Oregon. Walt and Roy could now afford to help their parents, and they urged the elderly couple to move to Los Angeles. When they finally agreed, Walt and Roy bought them a house near their own houses. Elias and Flora moved in during October 1938. A month later, Roy Edward, Roy's son, found his grandmother lying on the floor, dead. She had been asphyxiated by fumes from a defective furnace.

Walt and Roy took Flora's death particularly hard, since the move to Los Angeles had been their idea. Until the end of his life, Walt found it hard to talk about the tragic accident.

But in spite of the tragedy, Walt was very busy. Before *Snow White* was completed, he had begun work on two more feature films. Short cartoons were still being made by Walt Disney Productions, but Walt had lost interest in them. Mickey Mouse was the only exception. Walt still identified with Mickey. But the future of the studio, he was sure, lay in cartoon features.

The next venture in that field, Walt decided, would be based on an Italian children's story, *Pinocchio*, which is about a puppet who comes to life. The multiplane camera was now complete, and Walt wanted to take advantage of the realistic effects it could produce. When Walt held a story conference on *Pinocchio* in 1937, he told his animators that they had to make everything come alive.

"Mountains have gotta look as if you could climb 'em, houses as if you could walk through the front door," he said.

Leopold Stowkowski, conductor of the Philadelphia Symphony
Orchestra, worked with Walt on *Fantasia*.

The characters, Walt added, had to look real, too. The women who colored the drawings made by the animators worked out a method of blending colors that made the characters look soft and real. The new way of coloring, plus the strides the artists had made in showing movement in *Snow White*, produced the most realistic characters the studio had achieved yet.

But all the special work took time, and time was money. By the time *Pinocchio* was finished, it had cost over $2 million.

Pinocchio was in its beginning stages when Walt began planning a new role for Mickey Mouse. Walt still loved his mouse, even though his popularity had dropped. But children always asked Walt to draw Mickey, and adults still linked Walt with the famous rodent. How, Walt wondered, could he boost Mickey's popularity? Carl Stallings, who had worked at the Disney studio for a time, had brought a piece of classical music to Walt's attention. Walt decided Mickey would play the leading role in a cartoon based on the piece, *The Sorcerer's Apprentice*, which was inspired by a fairy tale.

During this period, Walt attended a party where he was introduced to Leopold Stokowski, the conductor of the Philadelphia Symphony Orchestra. A highly regarded conductor, Stokowski had just appeared in a film, and he was very fond of publicity. When he heard about Walt's plans for *The Sorcerer's Apprentice*, Stokowski offered to conduct the music for the film with his own orchestra. Walt accepted eagerly. When Roy heard the news, he was upset. Stokowski received one thousand dollars a night as a guest conductor, he pointed out to Walt, and his orchestra of one hundred musicians made fifty dollars an hour. Besides, Roy added, nobody cared about Mickey anymore.

But Walt had fallen in love with the concept of the famous one hundred-piece orchestra playing the music for Mickey Mouse, his own "alter ego." Still, he too was worried about expenses. So when Stokowski suggested that Walt expand the short by filming other classical pieces conducted by Stokowski and illustrated by Disney animators, Walt listened eagerly, his imagination taking flight.

A feature-length cartoon with cartoon characters moving to classical music would bring in far more receipts than a short piece. And no one had ever done anything like it before!

So the new film rolled ahead with Roy's reluctant approval. Stokowski, Walt, and the animators spent long hours in conference. Usually the music was chosen first and then the artists and animators went to work illustrating the piece. In the sequence on the creation of the earth, however, the idea came first and the music—from Stravinsky's *Rite of Spring*—was chosen to fit it.

It was a long, exhausting, and expensive process. When the two-hour film, now known as *Fantasia*—a "fantasia" is a free development of a musical theme—was finally completed, it had cost over $2 million, only slightly less than *Pinocchio*. But when Roy saw *Fantasia*, he was impressed. He even liked the sequence with Mickey Mouse. The public, Roy predicted, would make the film a success.

Walt agreed. All they had to do now, he told his brother, was wait for the money to roll in from *Pinocchio* and *Fantasia*.

But in 1939, World War II had begun in Europe. The Disney brothers quickly learned that the war, which was soon to involve the United States, affected their business. In Great Britain and France, proceeds from the films were "frozen," which means they couldn't be taken out of those countries. In Germany, Italy, and other countries that supported Adolf Hitler, the markets were now closed to Disney films. Before the war, the Disney films had done almost half their business in Europe; now all that business was lost.

When the two films opened in the United States, the critics loved *Pinocchio,* and so did many of the people who came to see it. But it was not as popular as *Snow White and the Seven Dwarfs.* A feisty little puppet simply isn't as appealing as a sweet young girl. The box office receipts from the movie's first run didn't quite cover its expenses. *Fantasia* was panned by most critics and box office receipts were slim. The film showed a big loss on its first run.

Walt was persuaded by Roy to have the two-hour *Fantasia* cut to eighty-one minutes. When it was released again, the film for which the Disneys had such high hopes was put on a double bill with a western. Walt had planned to make another film based on classical music. In fact, two segments of the film were already in production when *Fantasia* was released. Walt shelved his plans for it, although the segments already in the works were later used in other films.

"We still wonder what we would be working on today if *Fantasia* had been as popular as *Snow White,*" wrote Frank Thomas and Ollie Johnson.

Another film was in production at this troublesome time: *Bambi.* Based on a book by a Swiss author, it was the story of a young fawn growing up in the wild. All the characters were animals. The Disney artists were familiar with drawing animals for the short cartoons, and they already had one cartoon feature, *Snow White*, to their credit. *Bambi* should have been easier to do. But it wasn't.

The reasons lay in Walt's desire for realism in the cartoon. In the short cartoons, not much attention was paid to realism, either in the way the animals looked or in the ways they moved. Mickey Mouse, after all, was four feet tall! Walt wanted Bambi to be different. He hired an animal painter to lecture to the artists and he brought in live fawns and other live animals for the artists to study.

Doing the drawings the realistic way took a long time. Back when Ub Iwerks was turning out the first Mickey Mouse cartoon, he did up to seven hundred drawings a day. The fastest artists working on *Bambi* turned out only eight drawings a day. But the results, Walt felt, were worth it. Once, when he looked at the sequence in which a butterfly lands on Bambi's tail, his eyes filled with tears.

Bambi was the first Disney film in which all of the animators were not men. The Disney studio had artists on its staff who were not animators. Some drew sketches that were meant to inspire the animators and set the style for a film. One Disney artist, Retta Scott, excelled in drawing animals in action. When a realistic sequence with hounds was needed for *Bambi*, Retta worked with an animator to produce it and shared the credit with him.

Because *Bambi* took so long to animate, it was not released until 1942. It got good reviews, but it, too, made less than it cost to produce in its first run.

Walt in front of the new Burbank Studio.—Mark Wanamaker,
Bison Archives

Not all the Disneys' losses in this period were due to the films. When *Snow White* became such a huge success, Roy threw his usual caution away and borrowed $3 million to build the new studio in Burbank. At the same time that the new cartoon features were being produced at the Hyperion Avenue studio, architects and builders were working on the Burbank studio. Walt got involved in every facet of the planning.

The main building, the Animation Building, would be at the corner of Mickey and Dopey Streets (all the streets in the studio complex were named for Disney characters). Walt spent much of his time working out the details of this building, where his own office would be located. He even designed special desks and chairs for the animators. Up on the top floor of the building would be an area with a lounge, a gym, a sun deck, and a soda fountain; the first floor would have a snack shop.

Walt had also made drawings for an amusement park that would occupy two acres of the site. When expenses started mounting, he abandoned the plan. But he didn't forget it.

By the spring of 1940, the whole staff, which now numbered over one thousand, was located in Burbank. Later that year, Roy asked Walt to visit his office. The summons meant trouble, Walt knew. When Roy had good news, he came to Walt's office.

Roy talked for a long time, outlining the details of the Disneys' financial situation. They were now in debt to the bank for $4.5 million, he told his brother.

Roy must have expected Walt to be upset, but instead he exploded into nervous laughter. "Do you remember when we couldn't borrow a thousand dollars?" he asked.

Roy began to laugh, too. The brothers exchanged memories of the days when they had had to plead for small loans to meet their bills. But then Roy told Walt that they would have to go "public"—sell stock in Walt Disney Productions on the stock market to raise cash. Walt hated the idea; it meant he wouldn't be in full control of his own company. And control had been very important to him since he had lost Oswald. But there was no alternative if he didn't want to sell out to one of the large Hollywood studios. They had to have cash.

When the stock was sold, Walt and Roy and their wives kept large blocks of it. Some of these shares were given to the employees as bonuses.

Walt had laughed at Roy's concern over their debts, but actually Walt was concerned himself. To show that the studio could produce an inexpensive cartoon feature, he selected a modern children's story for his next film. It had a very simple plot about the ability of a big-eared baby elephant to fly. Work was started on *Dumbo* while *Bambi* was still moving slowly through the production process.

One day, when Walt was working in his Burbank office, his secretary announced a surprise visitor: Ub Iwerks. Walt greeted his old friend cordially, although the two had barely spoken for the past ten years. The visitor explained that his small studio had failed. He asked for a job, not in animation, but as a technician. Walt knew that Ub was a superb technician who had built his own version of the multiplane camera. He immediately offered Ub his own workshop at the Disney studio.

Ub was soon busy in the workshop, where he was to produce some of the brilliant technical innovations used in future Disney films. But he and Walt never became close again. Walt couldn't forget Ub's betrayal.

Ub arrived back in Walt's life at a time when the studio was undergoing big changes. The new surroundings were only part of the changes. Walt, now almost forty, was thought of by his employees, most of whom were young men and women, as a father—a stern father. Walt was quick to criticize, and he often launched attacks on an employee's competence in front of other employees. Most of them feared his hot temper. On the other hand, Walt almost never praised anyone. The only way an animator knew if the boss was pleased was if he mentioned it to a third party.

And although Walt was open to ideas in his story conferences, he tolerated no opposition once he had made up his mind. "You learned early on never to argue or cross him," said Ward Kimball, one of Disney's long-time animators.

At the Hyperion Avenue studio, the Disney employees had accepted Walt's drawbacks as a boss because they believed—correctly—that they were doing work that would change the whole nature of the filmed cartoon. Walt's abilities to inspire them made up for a host of shortcomings. "We all knew he was a genius," explained Ward Kimball. Even the rather modest salaries most employees received did not arouse much discontent. Walt and Roy did not live like Hollywood producers, and they plowed most of their money back into the studio.

The success of *Snow White* changed everything. The

animators and other workers believed that now they would be rewarded, not only with money but with recognition. Their names would be listed on all cartoons, short and long. But there were no raises, and Walt announced that only the long cartoons would list artists' names. The new studio only made things worse. At Hyperion Avenue, the employees had been crowded but they felt they were all part of the same team. At Burbank, Walt was separated from them. When they met in the halls, he never even nodded.

The employees, unaware of the Disney brothers' money crisis, felt neglected. Walt, preoccupied with his problems, didn't notice.

In 1941, Herbert Sorrell, the leader of the Screen Cartoonists Guild, met Walt in his office and claimed he had signed a majority of the cartoonists at Walt Disney Productions as members. If the Disneys didn't sign a contract with his union, threatened Sorrell, there would be a strike. For Walt, who hated any kind of opposition, these were fighting words. He vowed *not* to accept the Screen Cartoonists Guild. His lawyer backed him up.

When Walt came to work one day in May of 1941, there was a picket line in front of the studio. Only about 40 percent of the Disney employees went out on strike, but they included some of the most talented animators. Ub was not one of them; every day he crossed the picket line. When the two sides met for negotiation, the strikers' demands and their air of resentment horrified Walt. He was too emotional to make a good negotiator. The strike dragged on.

Finally, after nine weeks, the U.S. government came to the rescue. Walt was asked to undertake a trip to South

The strike by Disney artists in 1941 revealed long-standing resentments. One sign reads: "Are we mice or men?"—LOS ANGELES HERALD EXAMINER

America as a "goodwill ambassador," while mediators concluded the strike. Exhausted and angry, Walt agreed. While he was in South America, he received a cable that the strike was over. The Screen Cartoonists Guild had won. From now on, salaries would be negotiated by the union, and the credits of each animator and artist would be listed on all cartoons, short and long.

Walt received another cable while he was in South America. Elias was dead.

Before returning to the studio, Walt and Lilly attended the preview of *Dumbo* in New York City. The simple little movie, which had cost only $800,000 to make and ran just 64 minutes, was a big hit with both the public and the critics. It made almost $1 million in profits in its first run.

Back at the studio, Walt showed his bitterness over the strike. He closed the snack shop and installed time clocks everywhere. To anyone who would listen, he argued that the strike had been inspired by Communists. At one time Walt had supported Franklin D. Roosevelt, the liberal Democrat who was elected to four terms as president between 1932 and 1944. But after the strike, Walt voted only for conservative candidates who took a militant anti-Communist stand. He joined conservative organizations to further his views.

Walt was still brooding over the strike when an event occurred that made it seem almost unimportant. On December 7, 1941, the Japanese bombed Pearl Harbor. President Roosevelt declared war on Japan and Germany. Only a few hours after Pearl Harbor, the U.S. Navy was on the phone to Walt, requesting films on aircraft identification.

It was the first of many such requests from all the branches of the armed forces, as well as some government agencies.

The most famous war film Walt made was requested by the Department of the Treasury. The department, Secretary Henry Morgenthau explained to Walt, wanted a film that would encourage citizens to pay their taxes. Taxes paid for war bonds, and bonds paid for planes, ships, and other war materials. Could Walt finish the film before the deadline for filing income taxes, which was then March 15? It was late December, but Walt agreed.

By the time he reached home, he had an idea for a film starring Donald Duck, who by then was the most popular cartoon star at the Disney studio. Walt and a small crew of animators—many of the young men had been drafted—worked eighteen hours a day on the project. Soon Walt was back in Washington with a set of storyboards. He set them up in Secretary Morgenthau's office and explained the story. When the presentation was over, Morgenthau shook his head. He didn't like Donald Duck, he said.

Walt didn't like opposition, even from the secretary of the treasury. "I've given you Donald," he said angrily. "That's like MGM giving you Clark Gable!" Morgenthau quickly backed down, and Donald became the star of a film called *The New Spirit*. It was seen by sixty million people, and the Gallup Poll showed that 37 percent of Americans were more willing to pay their taxes because of the film.

By the end of the war in 1945, Walt had turned out some two hundred thousand feet of film for the war effort, all of it at cost. The only other films he produced during the war were short cartoons. When the war was over, Walt Disney

Productions owed the banks almost $5 million. The Disney brothers were right back where they had been just before the war—deeply in debt.

Preliminary work had been done before the war started on two cartoon features, *Alice in Wonderland* and *Peter Pan*, and Walt wanted to get back to them. But Roy disagreed. The studio couldn't afford to jump into two expensive, time-consuming cartoon features, he argued; they would go bankrupt. The two brothers argued for long hours over the subject. Before, they had always managed to reach a compromise on their differences. But this time Roy wouldn't back down.

One night, they wrangled until eight o'clock. Finally, Roy stalked out of the office.

The next day, Walt came to Roy's office. The brothers stared at each other, their faces grim. Then Walt smiled and apologized.

The two brothers agreed that Walt would postpone work on the costly cartoon features and concentrate instead on cheaper films that combined live action with cartoons. As Walt put it, "We're through with caviar. From now on it's mashed potatoes and gravy!" The best of these postwar movies, *Song of the South*, was based on the Uncle Remus tales and was about 70 percent live action and 30 percent cartoons. Unfortunately, it didn't make much money.

The short cartoons continued after the war, but with one big change. Walt no longer did Mickey's voice. His voice was too hoarse, he explained. A heavy smoker, Walt had a smoker's cough and his voice had grown hoarse. But studio employees shook their heads sadly when they heard the news about Mickey. Walt had lost interest in Mickey, they said. The famous mouse would never be the same.

Only one thing seemed to give Walt satisfaction in the postwar period: trains. He installed an electric train in a room next to his office. When animators Ward Kimball and Ollie Johnson, both train buffs, saw it, they invited Walt to their homes to see their own trains. Walt fell in love with the model train Johnson was building and decided to build one of his own. He enlisted the heads of the studio machine shop and carpentry shop to teach him how to make the train. From then on, he spent all his free time on the project.

Walt's daughter, Diane, remembers that during this period Walt took a box of wheels he had cast at the machine shop with him wherever he went. At Palm Springs, where the family vacationed, Walt sat in the sun, filing the wheels. At home, he spent three or four evenings a week in the shop he had set up. He seemed to forget his other problems when he was trying to solve some problem with the train. Lilly, who appreciated the peace of mind the work gave Walt, was tolerant of the train, even when Walt insisted on installing the finished product on the grounds of their new house in Holmby Hills.

The *New York Times* movie critic Bosley Crowther interviewed Walt at the studio during this period. Walt made him feel "sad," Crowther said later. All his attention had been concentrated on building a model train!

Walt and Roy examine desk on which young Walt carved his initials as a schoolboy in Marceline. The two brothers were visiting Marceline on "Walt Disney Day" in 1956.—MARCELINE PRESS

Chapter Six

But while Walt was playing with his trains, his mind was working on his problems. By the late 1940s, he had developed a plan for the studio's future. There would be no more films made up of short features, he told Roy. Walt Disney Productions would produce one feature cartoon every three or four years. Most of the studio's output would be live-action films, which were much cheaper to make. They had already made a good start with live action in *Song of the South*, which had more live action than animation.

As for the short cartoons on which the studio had been founded, Walt had decided to stop production on them soon. Short cartoons were simply too expensive to make.

Roy protested Walt's decision to make the costly animated features, but Walt won the argument. Walt, as Roy once told a reporter, had "stick-to-it-iveness." "I'm afraid if I'd been running this place, we would have stopped several times en route because of the problems," he admitted. So Roy visited the bankers again, and soon Walt had money enough to begin putting his new plan into action.

The studio had three feature cartoons in the planning stages, and Walt gave the signal to concentrate on one of them, *Cinderella*. To help the animators draw the characters, Walt filmed the entire script with live actors first. Photostats were made of action in the film, and the animators flipped through the stats to see how an actor moved. It saved time—and money—and made the action more realistic. Most of the critics liked the film when it came out in 1950, and so did audiences. It made more money on its first run than *Snow White*. "Our Cinderella year," Roy said of 1950, as the receipts from *Cinderella* began to roll in.

By now, Walt and his animators had developed a characteristic style of drawing, which Walt insisted be used in every Disney cartoon feature. The Disney cartoons of the 1930s through the 1950s are carefully drawn, realistic, and full of dramatic effects and tiny details. Most of the characters, human and animal, can immediately be recognized as "Disney" characters. This is just the effect Walt wanted to achieve. He wanted people to buy Disney movies the way they buy a familiar product.

The high recognition factor of the Disney characters made them particularly popular for merchandise. Disney dolls, trains, toys, books, comic strips, cards, buttons, play money, T-shirts, hats, lamps, bookends, and a thousand other items poured into the market and were eagerly bought by children and their parents. Each item was licensed by Disney, and each one meant a royalty for the firm.

While *Cinderella* was still being animated, Walt took a trip to Alaska. There he met two nature photographers, Al and Elma Milotte. Walt was impressed with the wild beauty of Alaska and he assigned the Milottes to make a film about it. When they started sending in their film, though, Walt didn't like what he saw. He telegraphed the couple to shoot fewer roads and mines and more animals. The Milottes moved their base of operations to the bleak Pribilof Islands and photographed the fur seals that gather there every year.

Walt was so excited by the new footage the Milottes sent him that he decided to make a short film called *Seal Island*. But when Roy tried to sell the film to the RKO salesmen who would distribute it to theater owners, he got a cold response. "They all say, 'Who wants to look at seals playing house on a bare rock?' " he reported. The salesmen's reactions weren't surprising. In 1947, when *Seal Island* was made, there *were* no nature films aimed at the public.

Walt managed to get the film shown in a nearby theater. It won an Academy Award for the best short film of 1948. It also made millions of dollars for Walt Disney Productions.

Walt promptly announced plans for a series of what he called True-Life Adventures. Over the next ten years, the Milottes and other photographers turned in miles of nature footage that the Disney studio shaped into films like *Beaver Valley*, *Bear Country*, and *The Living Desert*. Some of the later nature films were full-length features. All of them made money and some of them received Academy Awards.

But not everyone liked the films. The nature films, critics pointed out, used editing, music, and narration to interpret animal behavior in human terms. "It isn't true to life," said Bosley Crowther. In one film, for instance, two wild boars butt heads to the music of "The Anvil Chorus." The footage in the nature films was shot by nature photographers, but the films were put together by the same men who put together Disney's animated cartoons. They knew only one way to tell a story—Walt's way. Walt's way, however, resulted in exciting films. These films did give many people a look at a world they otherwise would not have seen.

A year after he received an award for *Seal Island*, Walt plunged into a completely different kind of "island" film: *Treasure Island*. Based on the Robert Louis Stevenson book, *Treasure Island* was the studio's first totally live-action film. Walt chose England as the location because the box office receipts from prewar Disney films were still frozen there.

Since these funds couldn't be taken out, Walt decided to go to England himself in the summer of 1949 and make a movie with those funds.

Almost immediately, he ran into trouble. The first part of *Treasure Island* takes place in England, but then the story moves to a tropical island. England simply doesn't look like a tropical island, even in the summer. Walt couldn't afford to take his crew to the tropics, so he did what he often did when he was confronted with a problem: he turned to technology. He used a special type of painting called matte painting to make tropical backgrounds.

The matte paintings in *Treasure Island* were the work of a young English artist named Peter Ellenshaw, who had done similar work for British director Alexander Korda. Ellenshaw painted tropical backgrounds on large, clear panes of glass. A camera set up about six feet from a pane photographed the actors and any props they used through the clear parts of the glass. On the screen, the actors and the props looked as though they were in a scene with whatever was shown on the matte painting.

Treasure Island opened in 1950, and it was another Disney hit. Walt used the money from *Cinderella*, *Seal Island*, and *Treasure Island* to complete his next two animated features, *Alice in Wonderland* and *Peter Pan*.

Alice had been started before *Cinderella*, but the studio had trouble with Lewis Carroll's tale about the little girl who goes down the rabbit hole. When Walt had made *Snow White*, *Pinocchio*, *Bambi*, and *Cinderella*, he had changed the stories to fit his own concept of the tales as they should appear on the screen. He wanted to do the same thing with

Sterling Holloway did the voice of more characters in Disney features than anyone else.

Alice in Wonderland, but everyone with whom he discussed the changes told him that a famous children's classic like *Alice* couldn't be tampered with.

So Walt let his animators follow the original story. The resulting film had some good scenes, but they didn't fit smoothly together the way scenes in previous Disney cartoon features did. Another problem with the film was the way it looked. Since Walt insisted that every cartoon feature be drawn in the same way, Alice and the odd creatures she met looked like Disney characters. But the book's original illustrations, which were done by John Tenniel, are almost as famous as the story. Many people couldn't accept Walt's version of Alice.

When the film became one of Walt's biggest flops, Walt wasn't really surprised. The character of Alice, he told people, lacked "heart."

Until *Alice,* Walt had depended mostly on unknown actors and his own employees for the voices of cartoon characters. In *Alice,* two well-known comedians of that era, Ed Wynn and Jerry Colonna, did the voices of the Mad Hatter and the March Hare, respectively. The man who was the voice for more Disney characters in features than anyone else, though, was character actor Sterling Holloway, who was first heard as the stork in *Dumbo.* His voice for the Cheshire Cat in *Alice* was one of the best things in the film.

The studio's next animated film, *Peter Pan,* which was also based on a familiar children's classic, did only a little better at the box office. By this time, though, the studio had more live-action films released, and all of them were making money. In 1953, when the studio completed *The*

Living Desert, the Disneys formed their own distribution company, Buena Vista, to release it. The salesmen they hired did so well that Walt and Roy decided to have Buena Vista handle all the Disney films.

Even though the studio was showing a profit in the early 1950s, they still owed money to the Bank of America. So Roy was far from pleased when Walt came to him one day and asked him for money to have plans drawn for an amusement park. Walt had talked about a park before, of course—it had been part of the original plans for the Burbank studio. Now, however, he was describing something much larger called Mickey Mouse Park.

Too expensive, said Roy.

So Walt took some of his own money and paid architects to come up with a plan for the enterprise. In 1952, he laid them proudly on Roy's desk. The park, Walt told his brother, would have only one entrance, which would bring visitors into a replica of a small American town at the turn of the century. Beyond the town would be a plaza with main avenues leading to four lands: Tomorrowland, Fantasyland, Adventureland, and Frontierland. Each land would have exciting rides for the children and plenty of greenery and benches where parents could relax.

Roy flipped through the plans, looking gloomy, and asked his brother how much it would cost to begin the park.

"Only a million dollars," responded Walt in his enthusiastic way.

Roy pointed out to his brother that Walt Disney Productions was now a public company; any large expenditure would have to be approved by the shareholders—and the

Walt couldn't convince anyone to finance his dream park.
—ANAHEIM PUBLIC LIBRARY

Bank of America. At Walt's urging, he reluctantly agreed
to ask the bank for financing. But the bank's answer, when
Roy relayed it to his brother, was a firm no. Walt erupted
in anger. Roy hadn't really tried to sell his idea, he charged.
But he was going ahead anyway. He would cash all his
assets to raise funds for Disneyland, as he now called the
park.

It was the most serious fight the brothers had ever had.
For a while they didn't speak, communicating only through
their secretaries.

Walt once told his daughter Diane that he wasn't pri-
marily interested in making money, the way some people
thought. "I think of money as a tool," he said. He didn't
want to bank the dividends he got from his Disney stock,
he explained; he wanted to keep the money "working."
When *Snow White* was a success, he had used the money
to make even more ambitious animated films. And when
his live-action films were a success, he wanted to use the
money to make something different—Disneyland.

Disneyland, however, proved even harder to finance than
a film. Walt threw himself into raising money for the new
park like a man obsessed. He set up a tiny company to
handle Disneyland's affairs and called it WED Enterprises,
for his initials. Then he cashed in his life insurance policies
and sold the house he and Lilly owned in Palm Springs,
California. Making the rounds of bankers and businessmen,
he showed them his plans and explained the merits of Disneyland. But even a superb salesman like Walt couldn't
arouse enthusiasm for his new project.

Everyone's reaction was the same. Amusement parks were
old-fashioned. Hardly anyone went to them anymore. And

although Walt argued that his park would be different, the bankers and businessmen shook their heads.

Meanwhile, the Stanford Research Institute, one of the planners Walt had hired, had found an ideal location for the park: 160 acres covered with orange groves in a town called Anaheim. But it was owned by 20 different families, and buying land from 20 different families could be very expensive. Walt had spent all the money from his insurance and the sale of his house. He knew he had to have at least $2 million more to get the project started. But where would it come from?

One night, while he was lying sleepless in bed, he found the solution. Television, he thought. Television!

Television was still new in those days, and there were only two important networks: CBS and NBC. ABC existed, but it was small and weak. Walt Disney Productions, like other film studios, had been approached by the television networks, who were seeking to buy films. In 1950, the Disneys had received an offer for their short cartoons. They turned it down, just as they had turned down the United Artists contract that involved television rights. Control had become very important to Walt.

But now Walt had a new idea. He would make films for his own television program, in exchange for the funds to build his park. When Roy heard about the plan, he liked it so much that he sent word to his brother that he would be willing to try to sell the plan to CBS or NBC. Walt agreed, and the breach between the brothers was healed once again. One of the Disney directors wrote a pamphlet on Disneyland that Roy could show to the networks.

It may not have been a very good pamphlet, or perhaps

Roy, Walt, and young Jim Payden fish in same stream the Disneys
fished as boys in Marceline. The Disneys returned to Marceline
for 1956 "Walt Disney Day."—MARCELINE PRESS

Roy was still not enthusiastic enough about Disneyland. At any rate, both networks refused to go along with the idea unless the Disney studio would make a pilot film to show what they planned to do on television. Walt, through Roy, refused. There would be no pilots. Not long afterward, Walt got a call from an executive of ABC. He offered Walt what he wanted: freedom to make any films he wanted on TV and backing for his park.

Walt agreed. That summer the first orange trees were removed from the site of Disneyland. A few months later, the Disney television show—called "Disneyland," just like the park—began its first season. Walt served as the host. At first he was nervous but he soon began to enjoy it. He was a good host: amiable, casual, and enthusiastic. Within a few months, the show was so popular that ABC had become a major network.

During the first seasons, Walt set the pattern for the show: a mixture of old and new Disney features and short cartoons, new feature films made especially for television, and films about upcoming Disney features and the building of Disneyland. Some critics complained that the films about coming Disney attractions were really just long previews, but the studio won an Emmy from the Academy of Motion Picture Arts and Sciences for one of them, *Operation Underseas*. It was about the making of *Twenty Thousand Leagues Under the Sea*, which was released by Disney in 1954.

The big hit of "Disneyland's" first year on television was a film about Davy Crockett, the Texas hero. Davy had worn a coonskin cap with a long dangling tail, and the star of the film, Fess Parker, wore the same type of cap in the movie.

The films were extremely popular, and the song sung in each film, "The Ballad of Davy Crockett," was frequently heard on radios and jukeboxes. In 1955, the three television films were released as a movie, *Davy Crockett—King of the Wild Frontier.*

Davy's coonskin cap was a natural for merchandising, but Kay Kamen, who had run the Disney merchandising empire so successfully, had been killed in 1949. His successor didn't see Davy's possibilities. Soon boys all over the United States were wearing coonskin caps, none of them sold through the Disney organization. At this point, Roy hired Vince Jefferds, a New Yorker, to handle merchandising. Jefferds blanketed the country with Disney versions of the coonskin cap, as well as Crockett rifles and buckskin jackets. Jefferds was soon making far more money for the Disney organization than even Kamen had.

In 1955, Walt introduced another television program on ABC: "The Mickey Mouse Club." Shown in the afternoon, it was aimed at children. The program included short cartoons, a daily serial with live actors, and newsreels about children's activities. But the most popular part of the "Mickey Mouse Club" was the Mouseketeers, a band of two dozen youngsters who wore caps with big mouse ears and bounded around the set, singing and dancing. One of the Mouseketeers, Annette Funicello, soon began receiving six thousand fan letters a month.

During this busy period, Diane Disney, the twenty-one-year-old daughter of Walt and Lilly, was married to Ron Miller, a classmate at the University of Southern California. The Disneys' younger daughter, Sharon, who was attending the University of Arizona, was Diane's maid of honor. Walt cried at the wedding. Ron Miller joined Walt Disney Productions and soon became a producer. A year after their marriage, the Millers had a son. Walt was a grandfather.

In Anaheim, Disneyland was slowly beginning to take shape. Walt had hired architects and construction engineers to actually construct the park, but employees on the regular Disney staff carried out much of the work, under Walt's direction. Disneyland was his concept, down to the smallest details. For some time, he had been spending most of his time working on Disneyland, and now, with the opening less than a year away, he was at the Anaheim site every day.

Disneyland, his long-term employees said, had become more important to Walt than films.

It was true. In an interview Walt gave to the *Hollywood Citizen News* at this time, he explained why. "The park means a lot to me," he said. "It's something that will never be finished, something I can keep developing, keep 'plussing' and adding to. It's alive . . . I just finished a live-action picture, wrapped it up a few weeks ago. It's gone, I can't touch it. There are things in it I don't like but I can't do anything about it. I want something live, something that will grow. The park is that."

But Walt the film-maker is very much in Disneyland, because Disneyland, as many people have pointed out, is a park made by a film-maker. It is laid out much like a movie lot with film sets. You can walk into the buildings, ships, caves, and other spaces, unlike film sets, but they are not quite true to life. On Main Street, for instance, which is Walt's idealized version of the Marceline, Missouri, he knew as a boy, Walt had every brick and shingle and lamp made five-eighths normal size.

There's another illusion, too. The first floor of every building serves as a shop or public area, and here everything is full size. But the designers scaled down the floors above, which nobody ever visits. The Santa Fe and Disneyland Railway, the train that carries visitors around Disneyland, is scaled down, too, as is the paddlewheel steamer *Mark Twain* that takes visitors down the "Rivers of America."

Walt checked all the scales himself. He often squatted down to child height and asked, "Can you see little kids looking up at this?"

Walt's film background shows up in the way Disneyland is laid out, too. He hated the way the exhibits at conventional amusement parks compete for the visitors' attention. At Disneyland, the visitor walking down Main Street sees Sleeping Beauty's castle looming up in front of him. The castle is an appealing object that pulls the visitor on to another attraction. Walking toward the castle, the visitor moves from scene to scene, just as happens in a movie. And when the visitor reaches one attraction, there are others in sight to move him on.

By mid-July 1955, everything at Disneyland was ready for the opening scheduled for Sunday, July 17. Before the gate opened, ten thousand automobiles had converged on the site, clogging every street for ten miles around. Thirty-three thousand people surged through the gates, thousands more than had been invited (counterfeit tickets had circulated for weeks beforehand). Some of the rides broke down.

Restaurants ran out of food. Water fountains ran out of water. There were so many people on the *Mark Twain* that water flowed over the deck.

The next day, many newspapers panned the park, just the way they had many of Walt's movies. "Black Sunday," Walt called the day.

But Walt was determined to make his new venture fly. He spent his days and even his nights at Disneyland, sleeping in the apartment he had made on the tiny second floor of the firehouse on Main Street. The food service, crowd control, and plumbing were improved. Traffic problems were worked out with neighboring communities. The park was made available to members of the press and their families on special evenings. Walt himself prowled through the park tirelessly, looking for problems.

Slowly it all came together. By the end of 1955, more than a million people had visited Disneyland, and most of them had gone away, as Walt had hoped, "with smiles on their faces." The park was able to pay off its loans by the time it was a year old. Each year, revenues grew. And each year, Walt Disney Productions, which soon purchased the shares held by ABC and another company, Western Printing, showed a better profit picture. The lean days were over. Disneyland soon made Walt Disney—and brother Roy—wealthy men.

Walt had been right again.

At Disneyland, Walt could indulge his love of trains. The Disneyland
train station is in the background.—ANAHEIM PUBLIC LIBRARY

Chapter Seven

Even when Disneyland was a huge success, Walt never tired of trying to make it better. No detail was too small for him. On his orders, messy items like cotton candy and peanuts in shells were not sold. A crew of maintenance personnel made constant circuits through the park, cleaning up bits of paper and other debris. After the park closed for the day, another crew hosed down the walkways and scraped up every bit of chewing gum.

Walt visited the park almost daily to check on the employees and the various attractions. Did an employee treat a visitor in a surly fashion? Walt told an assistant to give the grump a better understanding of the nature of Disneyland. Was a ride over too quickly? Walt cautioned the operator and later timed the ride himself. Was the artificial tree in the Tahitian Terrace too low? Walt had six more feet added.

On one occasion, Walt reprimanded an employee who parked his car near the Frontierland train station. The car destroyed the "illusion," he told the employee. Illusion is everything at Disneyland.

Walt made substantial changes in Disneyland after it opened. On opening day in 1955, there were twenty-two major attractions. Ten years later, there were over twice that many, including the monorail, which was added in 1959. Some of the attractions added in the 1960s involved a technique called Audio-Animatronics, which Walt originally developed for the New York World's Fair of 1964–65. There were four Disney-designed exhibits at the fair, some of which moved and talked and sang by means of Audio-Animatronics.

Walt had been fascinated with talking figures for many years, but earlier efforts to produce them resulted in relatively crude effects. Then, drawing on the technology used in the nation's space program, WED engineers came up with the solution: a magnetic tape that activated levers inside a figure by means of sound impulses. The system could move anything from an arm to an eyelid. Walt dubbed the system Audio-Animatronics. A Disney animator, Baline Gibson, whose hobby was sculpture, modeled the figures in which Audio-Animatronics was installed.

The Disney organization received four commissions from large companies to make exhibits for the New York World's Fair of 1964–65. Walt used Audio-Animatronics in several exhibits. The most popular was a figure of Abraham Lincoln who recited the Gettysburg Address—just as Walt had recited it in Benton School so many years before. Audio-Animatronics worked so well at the fair that Walt shipped some of the exhibits to Disneyland when the fair was over.

While Disneyland was being planned, built, and expanded by WED, Walt Disney Productions continued to make films. The studio released three new animated features between 1955 and 1961. *Sleeping Beauty*, the first fairy tale since *Cinderella*, cost more than any of the studio's other animated films. The multiplane camera created some splendid scenes. But the film lost $1 million and the critics panned it. Discouraged, Walt never did another fairy tale after *Sleeping Beauty*.

Luckily for the future of Disney animation, the two other animated films, *The Lady and the Tramp* and *One Hundred and One Dalmatians*, were hits. *Dalmatians* was the first

A family driving past an Audio-Animatronics exhibit at the
World's Fair, created for the Ford Motor Company.—FROM THE
COLLECTIONS OF HENRY FORD MUSEUM & GREENFIELD VILLAGE

film to benefit from a new invention of Ub Iwerks. He adapted a process so that the animators' drawings could be mechanically copied directly on the celluloids. Before, the drawings had to be painstakingly traced by the workers in the ink and paint department. The new process saved enormous amounts of labor and, of course, money. It also gave the animated films a looser, more flowing look.

Dalmatians looked different in another way, too. It didn't strive for strict realism, the way most of the earlier animated features had. The characters and settings had a kind of exaggerated reality.

The new animated films weren't the only Disney animated films available to the public. When Walt had formed his own distribution company, Buena Vista, to distribute his films, the company had begun a practice of releasing old animated features every few years. The policy was a big moneymaker. All the old films did well in rerelease, even the ones that had flopped when they were first released. When *Bambi* was rereleased in 1957, for instance, it cleared $2 million.

Rereleases and new releases kept Disney animated films before the public. But by the late 1950s, most of the films the studio was making were live-action films. The last short cartoons to be produced on a regular basis were released in the 1950s. Some of the new live-action films were excellent, like *Pollyanna*, but most were mediocre, like *The Absent-Minded Professor* and *The Shaggy Dog*. Many of these films were comedies that depended on some fantastic gimmick as the major plot device.

One night, when Walt had shown one of these films at

home, Diane told him how she felt about it.

"Corny," said Diane.

Walt told her that most Americans like corn. And, he could have added, so did he. He once said, "We're selling corn and I like corn."

Walt may have liked corny films, but another reason his studio produced them was that they made money. It cost so much money to make an animated film that the film had to do extremely well to cover the cost of production in its first release. But the live-action films the Disney studio turned out cost comparatively little, and they appealed to a large enough audience to give the studio a comfortable profit. Even a *bad* live-action film like *The Ugly Dachshund* made $6 million on its first release.

As he had in the past, Walt used his television program to promote his films. The program, which had moved to NBC in 1961, was still among the top ten. It was now shown in color, so that the films appeared to even better advantage.

By 1960, Walt was almost sixty years old. His thick hair and his moustache were graying, and the once-slim young man had become rather stout. He still smoked heavily, as his frequent cough indicated. But his major health problem in the 1950s was due to an old polo injury. It developed into arthritis in the neck area. Walt was often in pain. Hazel George, the studio nurse, tried massaging Walt's neck, and the treatment seemed to help.

Walt would visit Hazel's office every evening after work. She would rub his neck and back while he sipped a cocktail. Walt, who rarely confided in anyone, found himself confiding in Hazel during these sessions. According to Walt's associates, Hazel, a tough, sensible woman, could talk to Walt in a way no one else could. She teased him about his ego, which she compared to an ostrich egg, and she urged him to be more sensitive to his associates.

There's no evidence that Walt took Hazel's advice. Now that he was successful, Walt was even less likely to tolerate opposition than he had been before. Peter Ellenshaw, who joined Walt Disney Productions in Burbank in the mid-1950s, remembers one example of Walt's temper. Ellenshaw had been assigned to producing drawings for various films but he was anxious to return to his specialty, matte painting. He asked Walt if the move could be arranged.

Walt flared up immediately and told Ellenshaw in harsh terms that he was to continue his drawings. When Ellenshaw tried to speak, Walt barked, "I'm talking. You shut up."

Ellenshaw, Ward Kimball, Bill Walsh, and some other long-time Disney associates put up with Walt's moods and learned how to deal with their difficult boss. They did it because, as Ward Kimball once said, they thought Walt was a genius. None of these men ever became really close to Walt; Walt had no close friends. But they enjoyed friendly relations with him at work and sometimes visited his home. At times, Walt made warm and generous gestures toward these associates.

But some other employees could not take Walt's ego and his frequent anger. After Walt became successful, a number of talented employees left Walt Disney Productions to join other studios or to work on their own.

During these later years, Roy was one of the few people at the studio with whom Walt could really relax. The two brothers were "close—so close," according to Walt's sister, Ruth. Walt was loyal to those who were loyal to him, and he remembered that Roy had supported him—literally—in the dark days. Now that the sun was shining, he appreciated Roy's contribution to the Disney enterprises. Roy dealt with bankers and stockholders, the very people Walt always tried to avoid.

As for Roy, he knew who was the driving force behind Walt Disney Productions and WED Enterprises. "My brother made me a millionaire," he said once. "Do you wonder why I want to do everything I can to help him?"

In spite of their closeness, the two had frequent quarrels, which followed a predictable pattern. Walt would propose a scheme, Roy would throw cold water on it, and Walt would erupt in anger. Roy's family said that they could always tell if Roy and Walt had been quarreling by the way Roy drove into the driveway of their home. If the door slammed loudly as Roy got out, it meant Roy and Walt had been arguing. The end of the quarrel was predictable, too: Walt would apologize.

On one occasion, Walt wrote a note of apology to Roy, which he ended with the words "I love you."

At home Walt was often grouchy, too, but his marriage remained strong, and he and Lilly were both close to their daughters. In 1959, Sharon married and her husband, too, joined the Disney organization. Diane and Sharon would eventually give Walt and Lilly ten grandchildren. People who saw Walt with his grandchildren remarked on his fond-

P.L. Travers, author of *Mary Poppins*.—COLLINS

ness for them. Walt, in fact, seemed fond of all children. Even in his grouchiest moods, he was charming with youngsters.

Walt was charming with people he remembered from his own childhood, too. Every year, people Walt knew from his days in Marceline, Kansas City, and Chicago trooped through the studio on special tours. The high point of the tour would be a visit with the boss. Walt also took time out of his frantic schedule to travel back to the scenes of his youth. He visited McKinley High School in Chicago, the Kansas City Art Institute, and, of course, a number of sites in his favorite town—Marceline.

In 1960, Walt took up a project he had first considered when Diane was a child. Young Diane had a book on her night table and Walt picked it up. It was P. L. Travers' *Mary Poppins*, a story Diane and Lilly both loved. When Walt read the book at their urging, he thought that the eccentric English nanny who flies through the air with an umbrella would make a good subject for an animated film. Author Travers, whose first name was Pamela, was in the United States during World War II, and Roy had talked to her about obtaining the rights to her book.

Most of the authors the Disneys approached were thrilled to think that their book would become a Disney film. But not Mrs. Travers. She didn't like the idea of her character as a cartoon.

It wasn't until fourteen years later, in 1960, that Walt met Mrs. Travers in England and managed to persuade her to give him the rights to her book. At this point, Walt was more interested in live-action films than in animated films, and it was a live-action film that he described to Mrs. Travers. But she demanded a condition that Walt had never given to anyone else: script approval. In other words, she would be able to approve of how *Mary Poppins* was handled by the story department.

Walt was so eager to get his hands on the book that he said yes. Back home again, he threw himself into the preparations for *Mary Poppins* with an interest he hadn't shown in a film in years. It would be a live-action musical, he announced, but it would have cartoon segments using a new process developed by Ub Iwerks. Ub had found a way to blend live-action film and animated film so that it was almost impossible to see where the two merged. It was done by photographing the live action on a special screen.

The rest of the production staff was also made up of Disney veterans: Peter Ellenshaw, who did matte paintings of London scenes, Bill Walsh, who worked on the screenplay, and the Sherman brothers, who wrote the music.

Walsh found that a whole new plot was needed for the book, which is really just a succession of incidents. Bill Walsh was one of Walt's admirers, and it was his decision to make Mr. Banks, the father in the film, resemble the Walt Disney that Walsh admired. The father is strong-willed on the surface but underneath he is a soft-hearted man who gets along very well with children. He has another of Walt's traits, too: he has trouble with banks. Walsh made the bankers in the film the villains. Walt went through each draft of the screenplay, making detailed changes.

While the screenwriters struggled to adapt Mrs. Travers' book, the author herself arrived in Burbank. She read the latest version of the screenplay and objected to some of the changes that had been made. She also disliked the idea of songs in the film. A new version of the screenplay was produced and Walt, exercising his greatest persuasive powers, managed to get the author to accept it. But she remained unhappy with the songs. Why, she asked, couldn't they have some nice old songs like "Greensleeves"?

Everyone was relieved when she returned to England.

Walt had a preliminary script for *Mary Poppins* before he had a Mary Poppins. In the book, the nanny is middle-aged, and at one point Walt thought of using Bette Davis or Mary Martin. But Bette Davis can't sing and Mary Martin, who was on the verge of retirement, turned Walt down. Walt began thinking about giving the role to a younger actress. At this point, the name of Britain's Julie Andrews came up.

Julie Andrews, then a singer-actress in her twenties, was starring on the Broadway stage in the musical *Camelot*. She had played Eliza in one of the best-known musicals of all time, *My Fair Lady*. After seeing *Camelot*, Walt asked the actress to make a screen test for the Mary Poppins role. Miss Andrews was surprisingly reluctant. Later, Walt learned that the beautiful actress had made a bad screen test for the film version of *My Fair Lady*. She thought she wasn't photogenic.

Walt was so sure she was right for the role that he offered it to her without a screen test. She accepted—as long as she was not offered the role of Eliza in *My Fair Lady*.

Walt agreed happily. He had heard that the role of Eliza would be offered to Audrey Hepburn.

Julie Andrews thought she wasn't photogenic.

Audrey Hepburn accepted the role of Eliza, and Julie Andrews came to Burbank in February 1963 to star in *Mary Poppins*. Dick Van Dyke, the American comedian, played her friend Bert. The film proceeded smoothly but slowly. Live action was filmed first, on a special screen, and then the animators drew their characters to fit the movements of the actors. Walt was often around while the film was being made, looking for ways to make it better.

One day, Peter Ellenshaw showed the production team a dance he and his friends had performed in pubs during their college days. It was done to a Cockney tune, "Knees Up, Mother Brown," and involved prancing across the floor, knees raised as high as possible. When Walt saw Peter's performance, he insisted that everyone link arms and do the dance. "Get those knees up!" Ellenshaw kept shouting as the team pranced across the room again and again. Afterward, everyone was laughing, but Ellenshaw noticed that his boss looked tired and ill.

Walt liked the dance and tune so much that he promptly summoned the Sherman brothers and had the dance performed again. Could Richard and Robert do a song based on "Knees Up, Mother Brown"? he asked. The brothers nodded and disappeared. Within a short time they were back with "Step in Time," which became the basis for the sequence in which the chimney sweeps, led by Dick Van Dyke, dance across the London rooftops.

Mary Poppins had its premiere in Hollywood, at Grauman's Chinese Theater, on August 27, 1964. The audience cheered at the end. One member of the audience, however, wasn't happy. Mrs. Travers, who had been invited to the premiere, approached Walt. Julie Andrews was satisfactory, Mrs. Travers told Walt, but not Dick Van Dyke. He was too American! And she hated the dance numbers he did with the cartoon figures. The cartoon sequences would simply have to be cut.

Walt was too happy to be angry with the author. Fortunately, he told her, she had script approval only, *not* approval of the finished film. And when she read the notices, he added, she would love the film.

The notices—the critics' reviews—were everything Walt could have hoped for. They used terms like "superb," "magnificent," "irresistible," "sparkling," and, copying Mary Poppins' expression, "practically perfect." The chimney-sweep dance was hailed as one of the best dance sequences in film history. Critics who had been groaning about recent Disney films wondered in print how Disney had managed to bring off such a brilliant triumph. The film got thirteen Academy Award nominations and won five. One Oscar went to Julie Andrews for Best Actress. Another went to Ub Iwerks for Best Special Effects.

The film also made more money than any other Disney film—$31 million on its first domestic release alone.

The same year that *Mary Poppins* was released, Walt went to Washington to receive the nation's highest civilian honor, the Medal of Freedom, from President Lyndon B. Johnson. On his lapel, where President Johnson could see it, Walt wore a small button with the name of Barry Goldwater, the conservative leader. The citation for the award read: "Artist and impresario, in the course of entertaining an age, he has created an American folklore."

Walt receives the Medal of Freedom, nation's highest civilian award, from President Lyndon B. Johnson.—NATIONAL ARCHIVES

It seemed as though Walt couldn't top the year 1964. But throughout his life, Walt had refused to be content with his achievements. No sooner did he master something than he looked for another challenge. This time, the challenge was suggested by what had happened to his beloved Disneyland. Although the park itself was everything that Walt had hoped, the surroundings displeased him. Soon after the 160-acre site became popular, it was surrounded by motels, restaurants, and shops. Walt told a reporter that he couldn't afford to buy more than the 160 acres when Disneyland began.

"Believe me, if I ever built another Disneyland, I would make sure I control the class and the theme of the enterprises around it," he added.

"Control" was one of Walt's favorite words by then. One reporter heard him use the word twenty-five times in a briefing session with journalists. The Disney firm must control any project it undertook, he explained to the journalists. If they couldn't, they simply rejected it. Walt was now a millionaire many times over, but he couldn't forget the days when the Disney brothers found it hard to borrow enough money to produce their films. In particular, he couldn't forget Oswald.

He had lost control of the rabbit. It would never happen again—with anything.

As Disneyland became a huge financial success, Walt realized that he *could* build another Disneyland, and this time he *could* buy enough land to control the surroundings. Roy supported Walt's plan wholeheartedly. The brothers knew they wanted to attract visitors from the East Coast to the new facility, and Florida, which has much the same climate as southern California, seemed like the best place to build it. A number of studies of Florida locations were commissioned by WED. They pointed to a spot in central Florida near Orlando.

By this time, Walt not only wanted to build a theme park but something he called a "city of tomorrow." This would be a self-sufficient community with homes, schools, industry, and cultural attractions. Walt commissioned studies on city planning and spent hours reading up on the subject. He set aside a room next to his office for all the paperwork the City of Tomorrow generated and hired two men to work with him full-time on the project.

One day, Walt came up with a name for his dream city: EPCOT. It stood, he said proudly, for Experimental Prototype City of Tomorrow.

The studies Walt commissioned indicated that EPCOT, the theme park, hotels, and a housing development planned for an adjoining site would require some thirty thousand acres. In 1964, WED secretly began its efforts to acquire this vast amount of acreage. Secrecy was necessary because if people knew another Disneyland was planned for the Orlando area, prices would zoom upward and make it impossible for WED to acquire enough land. Walt himself didn't make an appearance in Florida until the purchases were well under way.

In the fall of 1965, though, the *Orlando Sentinel* newspaper announced on its front page that the Disney organization was the secret buyer of the Orlando land. By then most of the purchases were complete. Walt and Roy met

Florida Welcomes Walt Disney

WALT DISNEY   GOV. H

Walt, Governor Haydon Burns of Florida (center), and Roy at press conference announcing Walt Disney World.—FLORIDA DEPARTMENT OF STATE

with the then governor of Florida, Haydon Burns, and made the announcement of the new park, to be called Disney World, on November 15, 1965. In the press conference afterward, Walt mentioned the City of Tomorrow, but no one paid much attention to it. The glamorous new park attracted most of the attention.

Walt looked ill at the press conference, in contrast to Roy. Although Roy was eight years older than Walt, he now looked younger.

Back in Burbank, Roy and other Disney executives learned not to consult Walt too frequently about the new park. He just didn't seem interested. After all, as he pointed out, the new park would be just like the old one—but with more water. Walt even seemed to lose interest in his first love, animated films, during this period. The studio had one in production, *Jungle Book*, based on Rudyard Kipling's stories. After seeing some preliminary film prints, Walt said, "I don't know, fellows, maybe I'm too old for animation."

What he was interested in was EPCOT. Always impatient and demanding, Walt grew more so on the subject of the experimental city. His planners weren't moving fast enough. He snapped at them and he snapped at other employees.

One reason for Walt's bad temper, some of his close associates realized, was his health. Hazel George's massages no longer helped his neck pain. His cough was worse, too. Ward Kimball had a meeting with Walt during which he broke into a coughing fit that lasted for at least a minute. Hazel finally persuaded Walt to see a doctor about his neck. An orthopedic surgeon took X rays and found calcium deposits in Walt's neck. He also found something much more serious: a spot on one lung. Walt consulted a lung specialist at St. Joseph's Hospital across the street from the studio.

While the specialist's report was being prepared, Walt flew to the East Coast to accept another award. The report was waiting when he came home. There were suspicious nodules on one lung. Immediate surgery was recommended.

Walt held a meeting with his two chief planners for EPCOT. The plans, he told them angrily, weren't going fast enough. A few days later, Walt entered St. Joseph's Hospital. On November 7, 1966, surgeons operated and found a walnut-sized tumor on the left lung. It was cancer. The lung was removed. While Walt was in the postoperative room, one of the surgeons spoke with Lilly, Diane, and Sharon. Walt's prognosis was poor. He would live no longer than two years—probably less.

Walt was released from the hospital after two weeks. He was back at the studio the next day. Most of his time was spent in the EPCOT room. But by the end of the month he was back in St. Joseph's again. He spent most of his time in bed. Roy visited Walt on the night of December 14 and the two brothers talked about EPCOT. Walt pointed at the ceiling, which was covered with squares of acoustical tile. The tiles, he said, reminded him of a grid map for the Florida site.

Even though Roy knew about Walt's condition, Walt was so calm and confident that night that Roy felt his brother would survive.

Early the next morning, Walt died.

Roy (second from left) examines plans for Walt Disney World after
Walt's death. —Florida Department of State

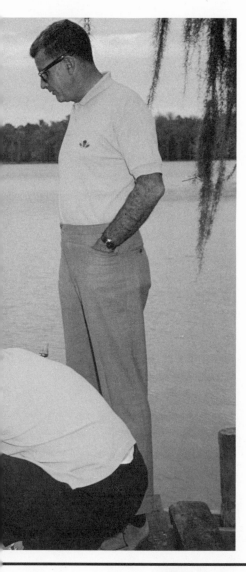

Chapter Eight

Roy traveled back and forth to the site of Disney World many times in the years after Walt's death. Finally, in 1971, the new theme park was ready. The official opening ceremonies took place in October 1971. A 145-piece symphony orchestra played music from Disney films while Julie Andrews and Glen Campbell served as hosts. Walt and Roy's families were there, including all fourteen grandchildren. At one point, an employee dressed as Mickey Mouse led Lilly on stage, where Roy asked her what Walt would have thought of the new park.

Lilly, wiping her eyes, said she thought Walt would have approved.

And he probably would have, at least as far as Disney World is concerned. The new park is really a bigger version of Disneyland, although it has some notable improvements. The most important is that the service facilities, such as the repair shops and the employee cafeteria, are located underneath the park in a giant basement. The basement is traversed by a network of tunnels, so employees can get from one attraction to another without walking through the park itself.

But Walt probably wouldn't have approved of some of the other things that happened—or didn't happen—at the corporation he created.

Roy's lack of interest in EPCOT, for instance. Roy ignored Walt's beloved model city, concentrating instead on bringing Disney World to completion. A few months after the gala opening, Roy died. He was seventy-eight years old. Ub Iwerks died the same year. The new president, E. Cardon Walker, a longtime Disney employee, knew how much

Walt wanted to make EPCOT a reality, so he had new plans drawn up for the experimental city. But the plans made EPCOT into a kind of showcase for American industry, rather than a new kind of city.

Walt might not have approved of some of the personnel changes at his empire, either. Ron Miller, Diane Disney Miller's husband, became executive producer at the studio after Walt's death. A cautious man, Miller kept turning out the same kind of films with which Walt had been so successful. The live-action Disney films of the late 1960s and 1970s looked much like those made before Walt's death. One of them, *The Love Bug*, was the biggest box office success of 1969. But most of the live-action films made after Walt's death didn't make much money.

The problem with these films was that while they remained the same, the audience had changed. Young people and families, who had made up the bulk of the Disney audience, wanted a different type of live-action film. Some of the big film successes of the 1970s were horror films like *The Exorcist* and science fiction adventures like *Star Wars*. The Disney studio tried to follow the trends, but most of its attempts, like *Watcher in the Woods* and *The Black Hole*, were poor copies of the originals.

People in Hollywood began to whisper about the Disney studio again. "The Mickey Mausoleum," they called it.

Luckily, Walt Disney Productions was no longer dependent solely on its films to make money. And while Disney live-action films were doing poor business, some other parts of the Disney empire were flourishing. Disney World, like Disneyland, attracted huge crowds. Rereleases

A giant figure of Donald Duck built by Goodyear floats above it all
in the annual Thanksgiving Day parade in New York City.
—GOODYEAR AEROSPACE CORPORATION

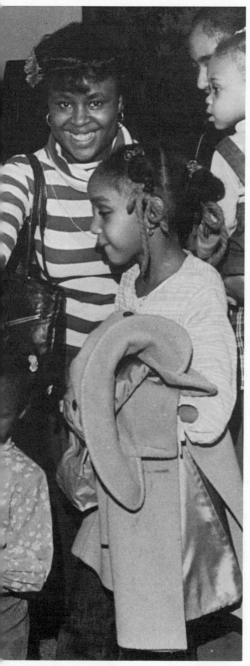

Mickey helps some of his young fans celebrate his fiftieth birthday in 1978 at the Library of Congress in Washington, D.C.—LIBRARY OF CONGRESS

of the classic Disney animated films played to large audiences, and so did new animated films like *The Aristocats* and *The Fox and the Hound*. Disney merchandise continued to sell, even though most of it was based on characters like Mickey Mouse who hadn't been in a movie in many years. But it didn't seem to matter. Mickey was more popular than ever.

In 1978, the famous mouse was fifty years old, and a number of museums around the country celebrated the event. At the Library of Congress in Washington, D.C., Mickey and his pals welcomed children and adults to an exhibit called "Building a Better Mouse." The Museum of Modern Art in New York held special showings of Disney cartoon classics and exhibited Mickey memorabilia.

Back at Mickey's home, Ron Miller became chief executive of Walt Disney Productions in 1980. By now the value of Disney stock had dropped and Miller realized that changes were needed. The board of directors approved the new plans for EPCOT. It opened in 1982 and quickly began to add to the company's profits. A new cable television channel, the Disney Channel, was started. A Japanese version of Disneyland—licensed by WED—opened and became even more popular than the American version.

And instead of asking the usual question, "What would Walt do?" Miller did something Walt wouldn't have done: he created a film company, Touchstone Films, to produce a new kind of live-action film aimed at a more adult audience.

Touchstone started off with a bang. Its first film was a huge hit: *Splash*.

But it was almost too late. Back in the 1930s and 1940s, Walt and Roy had gone from financial crisis to financial crisis, but today corporations with attractive assets are subject to the attacks of corporate raiders. The raiders acquire control of the corporations so they can sell off the assets, making huge profits for themselves. Companies with problems are particularly appealing to raiders. In 1984, Walt Disney Productions was attacked by a raider. The firm managed to fend off the attack, but it ended up short of money.

By then Roy Edward Disney, Roy's son and Walt's nephew, was unhappy with the way the company was being run. Roy owned more stock than any other individual, which put him in a powerful position. He suggested to the board of directors that the firm needed new leadership. In 1984, the board voted Ron Miller out of office and hired Roy's choice, Michael Eisner. Roy became vice chairman of the board. Eisner built a hotel and convention center at EPCOT, added new rides to both parks, made many classic Disney films available on videocassettes, and started a chain of Disney Stores to sell merchandise.

He also turned out a string of hit films for Touchstone. They include *Down and Out in Beverly Hills, Three Men and a Baby,* and *Good Morning, Vietnam.* Younger viewers haven't been neglected. In 1986, the studio released an animated film, *The Great Mouse Detective,* which reviewers said came closer to capturing the feel of the classic Disney films than any Disney film made since Walt's death. Eisner recently announced that from now on, the studio would release one new animated feature each year. That's a faster rate of release than Walt himself ever achieved.

Eisner's reign at Disney has been very successful. In the years since he took over, Disney profits have tripled and its stock is soaring.

Walt probably wouldn't have liked some of the things that have happened with his companies since he died. But the empire Mickey Mouse built now seems safe, and Walt *would* have liked that.

Index

158